AN OLD-FASHIONED
CHRISTMAS

AN OLD-FASHIONED
CHRISTMAS
American Holiday Traditions

text by Karen Cure

music selected & edited by Neely Bruce

menu & recipe editor, Lois Brown

HARRY N. ABRAMS, INC., PUBLISHERS, NEW YORK

On the half-title page: *Mandolin Christmas tree ornament.* Photograph by Bob Hanson

Frontispiece: *Victorian Christmas tree at Chateau-sur-Mer.* Courtesy the Preservation Society of Newport County

Right: Colonial Williamsburg Photograph

Project Manager: Lois Brown
Editor: Ruth Eisenstein
Designer: Darilyn Lowe

Library of Congress Cataloging in Publication Data

Cure, Karen.
  An old-fashioned Christmas.

  1. Christmas—United States—History. 2. Christmas cookery. I. Bruce, Neely. II. Brown, Lois. III. Title.
GT4986.A1C87   1984   394.2´68282´0973   84-3096
ISBN 0-8109-1816-1

© 1984 Harry N. Abrams, Inc., New York

Printed and bound in the United States of America

CONTENTS

INTRODUCTORY

The pages of this book retrace the long path from the first recorded Christmas celebration in America, that of John Smith in Virginia, in 1607, through Victorian times. They document the customs of bygone centuries—the decorations, the festive meals, the entertainments—particularly as they have been revived at some of America's great restored homes and historic towns and villages. In the festivities of yesteryear, whether of the earliest pioneers, or the hardy California forty-niners, or the comfortable Victorians, there is much to enrich the Christmas of today. Above all, the joyous traditions recalled here remind us that Christmas in America has long been a time of generous hospitality—of giving, of sharing, and of the gathering together of family and friends.

In Colonial Williamsburg decorated doors and windows express the spirit of Christmas past and present. Above the door of the Carter-Moir house the pineapple, the traditional symbol of hospitality since colonial days, is at the center of a fan made of apples, boxwood, and magnolia leaves. Colonial Williamsburg Photograph

FESTIVITIES 1607–1850

Colonial Williamsburg

Christmas in Williamsburg, the capital of His Majesty's royal colony of Virginia from 1699 to 1779, was a convivial time. "Nothing is now to be heard of in conversation," wrote a colonial diarist, "but the *Balls*, the *Fox-hunts*, the fine *entertainments*, and the *good fellowship*, which are to be exhibited at the approaching *Christmas*." With the crops safely gathered in, there was leisure for exchanging the latest news and gossiping with relatives and friends. Holiday visitors, often having traveled long distances, might stay for weeks.

Today's restored Williamsburg recreates the spirited activities of colonial Christmases against a backdrop of simple but striking decorations made of the natural materials available to eighteenth-century Virginia households. Bonfires are lighted, the Fife and Drum Corps parades along the Duke of Gloucester Street, ladies in crinolines and gentlemen in waistcoats and breeches dance in the Palace gardens, singers fill the air with ancient madrigals, and children play the old perennial games. Visitors to restored Colonial Williamsburg are invited to participate in the gentler pleasures of the Virginians of long ago.

Above: *The Fife and Drum Corps ushers in the Christmas season with a parade before the Governor's Palace (formerly the Williamsburg residence of seven royal governors and the first two elected Governors of the Commonwealth of Virginia—Patrick Henry and Thomas Jefferson).*
Colonial Williamsburg Photograph

Opposite: *A sport popular in Virginia two hundred years ago—shinnying up a "stout greased pole" to capture the bag of silver at the top—is still enjoyed at Colonial Williamsburg.*
Colonial Williamsburg Photograph

The wreaths and roping that grace Williamsburg exteriors during the Yuletide season are made up of a wealth of natural materials: apples, lemons, limes, pineapples, pears, pomegranates, and kumquats; dried okra pods, magnolia fruits, milkweed, sweet gum balls, bayberry, chinaberries, nuts, cotton bolls, mistletoe, and pine cones; holly, nandina, and pyracantha berries; ivy, cedar, balsam, pine, and boxwood; magnolia, aucuba, and camellia leaves. Even the window of the kitchen extension of the John Blair House makes a festive statement during the holidays.
Colonial Williamsburg Photograph

CELEBRATING IN EARLY AMERICA

Christmas in New England: Surviving the Puritan Ethic

In 1607, when "extreame winde, rayne, frost and snow" caused John Smith to keep Christmas "among the savages" with "more plenty of good Oysters, Fish, Flesh, *Wilde Fowl* and good bread" than in England, James I was marking the holiday with feasts and magnificent masques. English householders were decking their halls with holly and ivy, rosemary, and bay and laurel leaves. In kitchens, spits turned and ovens roared with the preparations for banquets of beef, beets, capons, carrots, fricassees, geese, parsnips, pheasant, salsify, turnips, venison, woodcock, a boiled wheat dessert known as frumenty (a forerunner of plum pudding), and Christmas pies.

A formal and elegant treatment of evergreen roping accented with bright red apples welcomes holiday guests to the George Wythe House in Colonial Williamsburg.
Colonial Williamsburg Photograph

On Christmas Eve in any one of London's Fleet Street inns, wandering minstrels and carnival showmen cavorted for the entertainment of boisterous crowds. The great Yule log was carried in and laid on the hearth, and the revelers danced before it as madly as the Saxons from whom they inherited their holiday customs.

Not everyone was enthusiastic about these celebrations, and the pro- and anti-Christmas factions that existed in England during the seventeenth century did not leave their arguments behind when they left for America.

It was the belief of the Puritans that the Church had no authority to prescribe practices contrary to, or not discussed in, the Bible. Since the Good Book did not ordain the feast days and saints' days—not even Christmas—the Puritans chose to ignore them.

The excesses of the English Yuletide celebration made the holiday a clear example of the "devices of men" and "suggestions of Satan" that the Puritans were taught to shun. So it is not difficult to understand why the Pilgrims were so resolute about spending Christmas as if it were "the same as any other day of the year," to use the words of Francis Beaumont, who traveled with the Pilgrims on the *Mayflower*. (The day was, however, differentiated for the sailors in the forecastle and the roundhouse: they had an extra allowance of sweet ginger for their noon meal.)

Reacting to the immoderateness of the English celebration of the holiday, the Pilgrims, upon arriving on American shores in 1620, "held grimly to their coarse diet, for fear they might make some concession to the ceremonies of the established church," and commemorated their first December 25 in the

13

Above: *Pendent ornament of carved-wood flowers, nuts, and fruits in an archway at Carter's Grove, a decoration inspired by the work of the famous eighteenth-century wood-carver Grinling Gibbons.*
Colonial Williamsburg Photograph

Opposite: *The mounding of a multitude of fruits, cakes, and cookies in pyramids or cones was the fashion in the eighteenth century. The apples, limes, lemons, grapes, kumquats, oranges, and pineapple are attached to a wooden cone with finishing nails hammered in at intervals.*
Colonial Williamsburg Photograph

New World not by feasting but by cutting down trees and splitting logs to build a storehouse.

Some of the very first laws enacted in New England forbade residents to "read the Common Prayer, keep Christmas or saint days, make mince pie, dance, play cards, or play on any instrument of music except the drum, trumpet, and Jew's harp."

In 1685, Judge Samuel Sewall of Boston noted with satisfaction in his diary that shops were open and farmers' carts were coming into town as usual on Christmas Day. The great Puritan minister Increase Mather spoke out in his "Testimony against several Prophane and Superstitious Customs" of 1687; in 1712 his son Cotton Mather decried the rowdyism associated with English celebrations in a discourse that has been called the first Christmas sermon ever delivered by a Puritan divine in New England.

But among the immigrants who came to Boston beginning in the late seventeenth century were some Anglicans, or members of the Church of England, and they celebrated Christmas well before the holiday gained widespread acceptance. In 1686 Governor Edmund Andros, escorted by two soldiers for protection, attended Christmas services—held in the Town Hall because no minister would lend his meetinghouse for the occasion. In 1706 there was a Christmas service in King's Chapel, but it was disrupted by a mob shouting names and breaking windows. The records of Christ Church, familiarly known as "Old North," note that the wardens collected alms for the poor at the door on Christmas Day of 1733. However, the church did not put up its first greens until 1783, and it did not have music for the holidays until 1788. After the Anglicans' King's Chapel burned, Old South Church members voted, in 1753, to open their church to them for services, provided their guests would forswear their accustomed decorations of spruce, holly, and ivy.

Yet in the latter half of the eighteenth century there was, according to the diarist John Rowe (writing 1764–79), general Yuletide activity—party-going, the ringing of church bells, and public feasting.

One of the country's first Christmas trees was set up in 1832 by Charles Follen, a political refugee from Germany who was teaching at Harvard College. He decorated his tree with bright-colored paper cornucopias and gilded and painted eggshells filled with

barley sugar, lozenges, and other popular sweets of the day; some seven dozen wax candles were affixed as illumination, and, miraculously, the only casualty was a doll's petticoat.

Finally, in 1856, Christmas was made a legal holiday in Massachusetts. Despite this, even as late as 1870 a Boston schoolchild absent on Christmas Day risked punishment, as did a workman tardy as a result of attending church services. And in 1874 the transplanted New Englander Henry Ward Beecher could declare: "To me, Christmas is a foreign day. . . ."

Christmas Among the Virginia Planters

After the first years of hardship had passed, the Christmas festivities of the colonial plantations of the tidewater area began to take on an increasing resemblance to those of the mother country. With the tobacco cured, the barns full to bursting, the pantries crowded with jellies and preserves, the smokehouses stuffed with bacon and hams, the cellars crammed with apples, potatoes, and turnips, and the fields too sodden or icy to be prepared for the next year's crops, December was a slack month in the agricultural year.

For two or three weeks, from the middle of December until Twelfth Night, on January 6, the typical Virginia country gentleman and his wife gave themselves over to entertainment. "All over the Colony, an universal Hospitality reigns, with full Tables and open Doors," reported the *London Magazine* in 1746. Aside from the household chores, the prime tasks of the season were chopping the prodigious quantities of firewood necessary to warm the rooms and heat the ovens, and decorating the house with seasonal greenery.

The decorating of the house was carried out with a lavish hand, as in Colonial Williamsburg today, where the emphasis is on the natural materials available to eighteenth-century housewives. Virginians probably embellished their doors with wreaths made up of spruce, apples, and pine cones, set off by shiny yellow lemons (perhaps brought from Lisbon). In-

Right: A posset pot. On social occasions the pot of posset, a hot beverage, was passed from one person to another, each drinking directly from the spout. This example was made in England, 1690–1710, of tin-glazed earthenware and is 10 inches high.
Courtesy The Henry Francis du Pont
Winterthur Museum

Opposite: Cherry-wood cookie stamps from the early 1800s; each measures about 2 × 4 inches.
Courtesy The Henry Francis du Pont
Winterthur Museum

doors they tucked bits of holly behind paintings and mirrors on the walls, as did their English cousins in earlier times. Imaginative householders may have decorated with snowy cotton bolls as well as the more traditional pine cones and boughs, magnolia and bay leaves, holly, cedar, berries, and nuts.

As soon as Christmas approached, invitations were dispatched to friends and neighbors, sometimes with a sprig of precious mistletoe tucked inside as a good-luck token for the coming year. Visitors, having traveled in great carriages over ruddy clay roads that in fine weather could be as smooth and hard as a ballroom floor, might stay for just a day—and then again they might stay for weeks. The days and evenings were filled. There were fox hunts for the active and billiards and cards for the more sedentary. At balls and parties everyone danced—minuets, cotillions, reels, and other country patterns, with a waltz now and then. If a planter was moved to render a tune on the harmonica, accompanying voices rose in song. The one fixed point of the day was three o'clock, when dinner was served.

A typical table set for dinner in early-eighteenth-century Williamsburg featured a cone-shaped center-piece made of apples piled atop one another and crowned with a pineapple, all nestling in a bed of holly. Or the center of the table was graced by an arrangement of tiny red-cheeked lady apples, pine cones, and boxwood forming an X around a handsome soup tureen and four elaborate silver candlesticks.

Festive meals of gargantuan proportions were consumed not only on Christmas Day but also on the days leading up to it. A wealthy family like the Carter Burwells, who built Carter's Grove in Williamsburg, doubtless feasted on a huge turkey roasted in the great brick oven, dressed with chestnut or oyster stuffing, and served with a garnish of grapes. It was not unusual for a family to polish off a saddle of mutton, a round of roast beef, a Virginia ham, and fresh pork or sausages or venison, with sweet potatoes, Indian corn, and an endless procession of other vegetables, as well as condiments such as jelled cranberries, spiced crabapples, tomato aspic, and kumquats. Other menus featured boiled beef, wild goose, partridges, spare ribs, salt fish and eggs, mutton stew, broiled or boiled pigeon.

17

Text continued on page 20

Winterthur Museum

A bountiful board was a mark of status among English colonials, and refinement in dining was diligently pursued by the early settlers even though they lived on the edge of the wilderness.

A full-laden and well-ordered table was the fashion, and balance and symmetry in the arrangement of the dishes to be set on the fine linen were subjects studied by ladies of even modest households, who were able to find instructions and diagrams in their cookbooks. An eighteenth-century hostess took great pride in her dessert table display, which would typically include a silver or glass pyramid centerpiece, sometimes supported by porcelain or alabaster figurines. It was not unusual for guests to be presented with as many as twenty-four desserts, some ingeniously devised (little cakes containing hidden mottoes, for example).

"Yuletide at Winterthur" splendidly recreates the traditions of early American holiday entertaining. In the magnificent antique-filled country estate of the late Henry Francis du Pont in the Brandywine Valley of Virginia, twenty-one areas are formally and elegantly arranged for such holiday functions as dinner parties, dessert and punch, musicales, entertainments, after-dinner games, and a hunt breakfast, and visitors are welcome to browse among these festive period settings.

Opposite: *An early-eighteenth-century dessert table in Winterthur's Vauxhall Room, featuring tarts, fresh and dried fruits, nuts, macaroons, and cakes. The wicker-framed dessert board at the center of the table raises the featured dessert—a Black Walnut Cake— above all the others.*
Courtesy The Henry Francis du Pont Winterthur Museum

The grand finale, an array of desserts, provided pecan pie, a wine gelatin doused with custard sauce, petits fours, candied orange or lemon rinds, fruit cake, plum pudding, *and* nuts. Fine ale (brewed on the plantation), port, and Madeira were downed by the gallon. Eggnog, that distinctive Southern concoction, was served from vast silver bowls surrounded by arrangements of fruit and greens. Every Southerner had his private recipe; George Washington and numerous other hosts from all over the Old Dominion favored spiking the mixture with a blending of rye, Jamaica or New England rum, and sherry.

On Christmas Eve, rounds of muskets were fired. And, as in Old England, the Yule log was brought in from the forest on an oxcart, carried into the house, and lighted with much pomp and ceremony in the big hall fireplace. A bit of last year's log, saved for the occasion, was used for kindling. According to tradition, tossing a sprig of holly into the blaze was sure to put an end to one's troubles of the preceding year.

Churches were transformed into bowers of holly, ivy, and rosemary, in accordance with the prescription of the old English couplet:

> Holly and ivy, box and bay,
> Put in the church on Christmas Day.

The children and the servants, who were entrusted with gathering the greens, found pine, shiny magnolia and cherry laurel leaves, red cedar, and rosemary in the surrounding woods. To the colonists attending holiday services the center aisle appeared, in the words of one eighteenth-century diarist, as "a very pretty shady walk," with the pews "like so many arbours on each side of it." The pulpit was so festooned with ivy, holly, and rosemary that one wit took the occasion to say that the congregation "heard The Word out of a bush, like Moses."

On Christmas Day, more muskets were fired, the children were given small presents, and the servants, who made the rounds greeting everyone with the words "Christmas gift!" received extra rations and small presents of money. Philip Vickers Fithian, the Yankee tutor to one highborn Virginia family in the eighteenth century, wrote in his account of his first Christmas in Virginia that the young boy who

Above: *Winterthur's grand Montmorenci stair hall, festooned with evergreens, and an inviting punch table. Punch was particularly popular at Christmastime in early America; it was served to the gentlemen as well as to the ladies, from the midday meal into the late evening.*
Courtesy The Henry Francis du Pont Winterthur Museum

Below: *An eighteenth-century setting for an after-the-ball buffet in Winterthur's Marlboro Room. Christmas was a popular time for courting and for weddings. Both George Washington and Thomas Jefferson were married during the holiday season.*
Courtesy The Henry Francis du Pont Winterthur Museum

customarily made his fire, blacked his boots, and did his errands "was early in my Room, drest only in his shirt and Breeches!" Fithian, having been apprised of the local custom, gave him a few cents. Soon afterward, before he was dressed, the boy assigned to take care of his schoolroom fires appeared, made three or four "profound bows," extended *his* holiday greeting—and received *his* few coins. Then another boy appeared, and Fithian handed over a few more coins. By the time he was next greeted, he had to resort to IOUs.

Christmas trees were not a feature of the Virginia celebrations until the middle of the nineteenth century. One of the first on record was set up in 1842 in Williamsburg by a German-born instructor at the College of William and Mary, Charles Minnegerode. He used wire to affix the candles and trimmed his creation with popcorn, nuts, ornaments made from colored paper, and a gold star.

Christmas in Old New York

The Dutch burghers of old New York offer a holiday picture vastly different from that of their sterner neighbors to the north, the Puritans. Not only did they celebrate Christmas Day; they made it the climax of a whole season of merrymaking. Unconstrained by the presence of a handful of Puritans in the colony, they began frolicking and feasting on St. Nicholas' Eve, December 5, and let the festive spirit rule until after Christmas Day.

Thus on December 14, 1654, the town fathers canceled their council meetings for three weeks. Commerce ground to a halt, but confectionery stores and toy shops were open, festooned with bright silk drapery, flowers, and evergreens. Dutch housewives polished their brass, copper, pewter, and silver, sanded their floors, roasted turkeys, and baked mammoth quantities of cakes, pies, and puddings. Houses and churches were decorated with evergreens—and stayed that way through Candlemas, on February 2.

From Dutch times on, during the Yuletide season there were scores of social gatherings in New York. In 1800, when Harriet and Maria, the daughters of Connecticut's Governor Jonathan Trumbull, visited the city over the holidays, they wrote home of

receiving "sweet Christmas kisses," for kissing games were an outstanding feature of every affair. Occasionally, of an evening, young men stole away from home and, in groups of five or six, guided by the twinkling light of lanterns, perambulated from house to house singing Christmas carols to the accompaniment of horns and perhaps a fiddle.

For children, one of the main features of the season was the arrival of St. Nicholas, weighted down with books, cakes, fruits, and toys for virtuous little boys and girls. Scarcely a child did not mind his manners as Christmas approached, and on St. Nicholas' Eve, each one would fill his shoes with hay and a carrot or two for the white horse that the good saint was known to ride from house to house.

Washington Irving, in *A History of New York*, penned in 1809 under the pseudonym Diedrich Knickerbocker, virtually rewrote history by describing how Dutch children hung stockings on St. Nicholas' Eve, rather than setting out shoes. He also described how the generous old saint rode high above the trees and left his famous white horse and his wagon parked on rooftops while he slid down chimneys to deliver his bounties. Irving also originated the image of St. Nicholas laying a finger beside his nose before flying off into the sky.

About a decade later, in 1821, a small Christmas book, *The Children's Friend: A New-Year's Present, to Little Ones Five to Twelve*, with colored engravings, depicted not a wagon but a sleigh, pulled not by a horse but by reindeer; gifts were brought for the good children and switches for those who had been bad, on Christmas Eve rather than St. Nicholas' Eve. The driver of the sleigh was a diminutive "Santeclaus"— the name derives from the Teutonic Sanct Herr Nicholaas and the Dutch Sintirklass. Some of the same imagery appeared in the famous poem "A Visit from St. Nicholas," later better known as "Twas the Night Before Christmas," generally attributed to a New York City professor of biblical studies named Clement Clarke Moore, and first published in 1823. The poem added to the previously published descriptions of St. Nick's holiday doings by enumerating and naming his reindeer and by transforming him into the familiar "jolly old elf" with the "little round belly that shook, when he laughed, like a bowl full of jelly."

Not far away from New York, in the communi-

The dining table in Winterthur's Queen Anne Room is set for dessert in the eighteenth-century English "crowded" fashion. Paired pyramids of grapes and lady apples flank a two-tiered glass dish offering syllabubs, almond and pistachio creams, sugared violets, and mint leaves.
Courtesy The Henry Francis du Pont Winterthur Museum

ties around Lancaster, Pennsylvania, the children of German immigrants believed that on Christmas Eve the Christ Child (the name took many forms, from Christkindel to Krist-Kringle) traveled on muleback through the land and entered houses through the keyhole to leave gifts. To receive these, children hung stockings or left straw baskets or soup plates on the dining table. This gift-bringer acquired a whole series of progressively more anglicized names before finally becoming Kriss Kringle, the figure who made his debut in *Kriss Kringle's Book*, published by Thomas Cowperthwaite & Co., in 1842, and who appeared again three years later in *Kriss Kringle's Christmas Tree: A Holiday Present for Boys and Girls*, published by another Philadelphia concern, E. Ferrett & Co.

By the time these books appeared, the ideas of Washington Irving and Clement Clarke Moore about a jolly old elf with a white beard and a fur-trimmed hat and coat had spread so far that publishers ignored the mule, the keyhole, the soup plates, and all the other local concepts associated with the German Christkindel, except for the name. *Kriss Kringle's Christmas Tree* had the gifts being put not in shoes or stockings but on the Christmas tree. And since this Kriss Kringle was hugely successful and widely advertised, it was not long before children who had heretofore looked to their stockings or their shoes or their plates for their holiday booty began expecting to find it tucked between the branches of the Christmas tree.

Immigrants arriving in New York, Philadelphia, and other coastal ports, anxious to take on the customs of their new land, adopted the image. The jolly old elf's commercial fame was assured when large stores began advertising themselves as "Kriss Kringle's Headquarters" and hiring a Kriss Kringle/Santa Claus/St. Nicholas to drum up business among children and their parents. All that remained to complete the evolution of the jolly old elf that we know today was for the political cartoonist Thomas Nast, working in New York, to give him standard features and dimensions—as he did in his series of annual Christmas illustrations for *Harper's Weekly Magazine* from 1863 until 1886. But that's getting ahead of the story.

New Year's Day, which generally marked the end of the holiday merrymaking, was also important in Dutch New York. In honor of the holiday, merchants signified their good will to their customers with some special token (the baker's dozen was traditional). The ladies of every house donned their best gowns to receive callers, and huge bowls of punch were set out, with immense platters of plain cookies, the distinctively Dutch doughnuts known as *oleykoeks*, and, sometimes, the finest of imported European cookies. The fare became grander as New York's prosperity increased, and by the 1840s New Year's Day callers enjoyed, in the words of a contemporary observer, "splendid ornamented and iced plum cakes, with almost numberless other cakes, confectionaries, and fruits, not forgetting the true New Year's Cakes, together with Madeira and other wines, and cordials, and liquors."

Christmas in and around Philadelphia

In America's earliest years it was the larger population centers, where the proportion of wealthy merchants and professionals—and Anglicans—was high, that saw the most widespread and most festive Yuletide merrymaking. And so it was that in Philadelphia and nearby areas of eastern Pennsylvania the celebrations were almost as hearty as in New York—despite the fact that many citizens were Quakers and, until as late as 1862, habitually referred to December 25 as "the day called Christmas."

In 1851 the *Philadelphia Sun's* New York correspondent reported that although New York was more festive on New Year's Day, Philadelphia surpassed it by far in the celebration of Christmas. In the City of Brotherly Love the Legislature recessed for an extended Christmas holiday. Church bells rang, and there was much imbibing of eggnog. Evening parties were the mode. Hostesses served terrapins, oysters, and calves'-foot jelly, and there was ice cream for dessert. Brandy, champagne, hock, and claret punch were the beverages. One account of a party in 1744 mentioned a punch bowl large enough for half a dozen young geese to swim in. Newspaper reporters wrote of "the sunny, joyous, full-fed" faces of Philadelphians on Christmas Day. People went to church, both before and after dinner. But religious obligations by no means took precedence over social amenities.

Perhaps in order to stir up interest among congregations who took their religion lightly, churches

Text continued on page 29

During the holidays, cookies molded in fancy shapes were often displayed in the windowpanes of rural Pennsylvania-German homes to amuse and impress passersby. After the 1850s such cookies were usually colored.
Courtesy The Henry Francis du Pont Winterthur Museum

Sunnyside, Washington Irving's home from 1837 to 1859. Courtesy Sleepy Hollow Restorations

Sleepy Hollow Restorations

The spirit of an early-nineteenth-century Christmas in New York is conveyed in a letter that Washington Irving, America's first great literary figure—creator of Rip Van Winkle and Ichabod Crane—wrote to his niece:

> There we are in the Christmas holydays; the cottage dressed in evergreens and enlivened by cheerful voices. . . . We have passed a pleasant Christmas day. It does not take much to make a fete in our simple establishment. We had [guests] to dine and pass the evening with us; there was music and dancing and all seemed to enjoy themselves.

Each year, three centuries of Christmas traditions are faithfully recreated at the Sleepy Hollow Restorations in New York. The historic sites of Sunnyside, Washington Irving's home in Tarrytown; Philipsburg Manor, an early-1700s Dutch-American grist mill and trading center in North Tarrytown; and Van Cortlandt Manor, a great estate dating to the 1680s, in Croton-on-Hudson, are decorated for the holidays precisely as they would have been in their day. At these gracious restorations traditional holiday food is prepared, and in keeping with the long American tradition of hospitality, the public is invited to participate in holiday fare, candlelight tours, and music.

Opposite: *The fireplace at Sunnyside, with Christmas stockings hung from the mantel. "St. Nicholas rode among the tree tops, or over the roofs of houses, now and then drawing forth magnificent presents from his breeches' pockets, and dropping them down the chimneys of his favorites." —Washington Irving, 1809.*
Courtesy Sleepy Hollow Restorations/
Early American Life Magazine

Right: *A huge "kissing bell," made up of greens, apples, oranges, candles, and mistletoe, hangs in the entranceway of the Van Cortlandt Manor during the Christmas season.*
Courtesy Sleepy Hollow Restorations/
Early American Life Magazine

vied with one another to offer the finest music. When the Swedish traveler Peter Kalm visited Philadelphia in 1750, he found that it was the "papal place of worship," with its violinists and singers, that had become the favorite, attracting, both for high mass and for vespers, not only its own members but also citizens of other faiths. There, and elsewhere, the pews and altar were decorated with laurel, and evergreen garlands festooned the chancel railings and entwined the columns supporting the pulpit as well as the elaborate carving of the pulpit itself.

As late as 1825, Christmas trees were uncom-mon in Philadelphia. According to the *Saturday Evening Post* of December 10, 1825, Christmas trees were visible through the windows of some houses, their green boughs "laden with fruit, richer than the golden apples of the Hesperides, or the sparkling diamonds that clustered on the branches in the wonderful cave of Aladdin." The extravagance of this description may be due at least in part to the trees' rarity. They were so infrequently seen that at one of the ladies' bazaars held about 1830 a "famous CHRISTMAS TREE" was exhibited, with an admission charge of 6¼ cents. Four years later trees were

Christmas sweets, holiday greens, and fine china at Washington Irving's Sunnyside.
Courtesy Sleepy Hollow Restorations/*Early American Life Magazine*

still a curiosity, and when the German-born Dr. Constantin Hering carried an evergreen he had cut in New Jersey through Philadelphia in 1834, he attracted a crowd of curious young onlookers who had heard about the wondrous phenomenon, no doubt in the *Saturday Evening Post.*

Anglican residents of the area had brought from England the custom of Christmas Eve mumming, and groups of masked performers often promenaded from house to house, presenting bits of impromptu theater and collecting a few pennies or seasonal sweets for their efforts as they chorused:

> Christmas is coming, geese are getting fat.
> Please put a penny in the old man's hat.
> If you haven't got a penny, a ha'penny will do;
> If you haven't got a ha'penny, God bless you!

Quantities of old-fashioned Christmas cookies are baked in the old-fashioned kitchen at Sunnyside.
Courtesy Sleepy Hollow Restorations/*Early American Life Magazine*

Sometimes their drumbeating and noisemaking awakened quiet Quaker souls like Elizabeth Drinker, who complained in her diary in 1805 about a "dull heavy thumping" she could not at first account for—"a Kittle-drum, a strange way of keeping Christmas"—that she heard at about one o'clock in the morning, "a disagreeable noise in my ears."

With such goings on throughout the city, even Quakers could not ignore the holiday spirit. Though they never decorated their houses with spruce or hemlock, by this time Quakers had become accustomed to such Christmas fare as stuffed turkeys and mince pies, and they looked "quite as full and as fat and as rosy and as happy, and as satisfied with the inner man, as the devotées of the green boughs," according to a report in a newspaper of 1847.

Out in the countryside, it was the Pennsylvania "Gay" Dutch—the Lutherans and the members of the Dutch Reformed Church—who set the holiday's tone. The Christmas tree was central to the Pennsylvania Dutch celebration of the holiday as early as 1821—before the custom was adopted by any other group. Selecting the tree in the forest, cutting it, bringing it home, and decorating it were all part of the traditional family country Christmas. The trimmings—gingerbread cut into shapes, strings of raisins and apples, bright-colored flannel rosettes, festoons of almonds, tiny baskets filled with nuts, peanuts and pretzels, blown-out eggshells embellished with strips of bright-colored paper—were the forerunners of a spectacular array yet to come.

In the early days, when life was still relatively simple, women baked only one kind of cookie, usually the spicy lebkuchen, and any housewife who ventured to make as many as two kinds of Christmas cookies ran the risk of being considered "big-notioned," as one old-timer reminisced. Cookies were shaped with cookie cutters fashioned by the local tinsmith and were baked by the score: birds, fish, moons, pigs, rabbits, horses, stars, trees, tulips, and hearts of all sizes. Each housewife had her collection, and neighbors made exchanges, but every cookie baker liked to have one shape that was unique to her. Toward the middle of the nineteenth century, eggy, anise-seasoned springerle made with intricate wooden molds skillfully carved in Germany from soft-grained pear- or boxwood became a favorite cookie.

Holiday music at Sunnyside.
Courtesy Sleepy Hollow Restorations/*Early American Life Magazine*

Confectioners baked fruitcakes, plum cakes, and Dutch cakes—each baker vying for the honor of turning out the largest cake. In the contest, pastries as large as wagon wheels were produced. When company came, all these delectable sweets, homemade and bought, were placed on a side table, flanked by a huge pitcher of cider and baskets of walnuts, hickory nuts, and chestnuts—and Christmas hospitality reigned.

Text continued on page 48

Above: *On the hearth are wooden shoes filled with carrots and straw for the horse that carries St. Nicholas and his gifts to the children of the house.*
Courtesy Sleepy Hollow Restorations/*Early American Life Magazine*

Opposite: *A traditional eighteenth-century Christmas dinner in the mid-Atlantic states is featured in Winterthur's Vauxhall Room. A roast suckling pig is the center of attention, complemented by a chicken pie. Silver tankards will contain ale or beer, while a Delft tureen on the dressing table holds onion soup. In the absence of refrigeration, the vegetables and fruits would have been those easily dried or salted.*
Courtesy The Henry Francis du Pont Winterthur Museum

The menu for the **Early American Yuletide Feast** *combines recipes from* Yuletide at Winterthur: Tastes and Visions of the Season *(a Winterthur Book, © 1981) and from* The Williamsburg Cookbook *(Colonial Williamsburg Foundation, © 1971).*
    A festive early American meal would have included an astonishing variety of main dishes and desserts, including steak, chicken pie, goose, oysters, turnips, green beans, puddings, gingercakes, . . . "everything which could delight the eye or allure the taste," said John Adams in 1776, "curds and creams, jellies, sweetmeats of various sorts, twenty sorts of tarts, fools, trifles, floating islands, whipped sillibub &c., &c., Parmesan cheese, punch, wine, porter, beer, etc."

An Early American Yuletide Feast

Syllabub   Eggnog   Posset   Raspberry Shrub

Mulled Cider   Wassail

———————

Wigs

Spoon Bread

Cream of Peanut Soup   Oyster Stew

Wine Jelly Mold with Custard Sauce

Virginia Ham and Brandied Peaches   Chicken Pie   Roast Suckling Pig

———————

Plum Pudding   Fruitcake   Shrewsbury Cakes   Honey Cookies

Jumbles   Candied Rose Petals

To make whipt Syllabubs

A festive concoction that can either be sipped from a cup or eaten from a dish with a spoon, syllabub is perhaps so named from the wine of Sillery, in the Champagne region of France, and from bub, Elizabethan slang for a frothing drink.

Mix cream with 1 tablespoon of the sugar and grated lemon peel. Whip until stiff peaks form. Gently stir in wine. Beat egg whites until stiff, add remaining tablespoon of sugar, beat well, and fold into whipped-cream mixture. Place in small cups or glasses. Chill for at least an hour. Makes six servings.

1 cup heavy cream
2 tablespoons sugar
peel of 1 lemon, grated
½ cup white dessert wine
3 egg whites

—*Yuletide at Winterthur*

Eggnog

Beat egg yolks with sugar until thick. Slowly add bourbon and cognac. Mix in cream and chill several hours. Whip egg whites with salt until they stand in stiff peaks, then carefully fold in the egg yolk mixture. Top each serving with a grating of nutmeg. Makes forty servings.

12 eggs, separated
1 cup sugar
1 cup bourbon
1 cup cognac
3 pints whipping cream
½ teaspoon salt
nutmeg

—*The Williamsburg Cookbook*

To make a Posset with Ale
King William's Posset

Posset, although closely related to eggnog, was made with ale or the dry Spanish wine called sack and served hot. It is also known to have been made with spirits and even hard cider.

Combine eggs, sugar, and nutmeg in a large, heavy saucepan and stir in the milk gradually. Cook the mixture slowly over low heat, stirring constantly, until it coats a metal spoon. Do not let it boil. When it is thick, remove from the heat and gently stir in ale or sherry. Serve at once as a hot drink or chill thoroughly and serve cold. Makes eight to ten servings.

6 eggs, beaten
½ cup sugar
½ teaspoon nutmeg
3 cups milk
1 cup ale or dry sherry

—*Yuletide at Winterthur*

Raspberry Shrub

A shrub (the word is derived from the Arabic sharāb, meaning drink) is a beverage made from a fruit syrup to which water, wine, or hard liquor has been added. In the eighteenth and nineteenth centuries, shrubs were used for medicinal purposes as well as for refreshment.

Swirl raspberries in blender. Strain juice. Put one cup of the juice in a saucepan, add sugar, and simmer until sugar is dissolved. Add vinegar and chill. Before serving add wine or rum. To serve, pour about ½ cup over ice in a tall glass. Fill to top with soda water and garnish with fresh mint. Makes about six servings.

—Yuletide at Winterthur

1 package frozen
    raspberries, thawed
1 cup sugar
¼ cup white-wine vinegar
1 cup dry white wine or
    white rum
1 quart soda water
sprigs of fresh mint

Mulled Cider

Mix all ingredients and bring just to a boil. Cool and strain. Then reheat, and serve hot with a cinnamon stick in each cup. Makes about sixteen half-cup servings.

—Yuletide at Winterthur

2 quarts cider
½ cup orange juice
¼ cup lemon juice
2 tablespoons sugar
3 cinnamon sticks
2 teaspoons whole cloves
1 teaspoon nutmeg

Wassail

Wassailing is an ancient English custom that has been revived in Colonial Williamsburg. The master of the English household drank the health of those present with a bowl of spiced ale, and each in turn after him passed the bowl along and repeated the Saxon phrase Wass hael, "Be whole," or "Be well."

Boil sugar, cinnamon sticks, and 3 lemon slices in ½ cup water for 5 minutes and strain this syrup. Heat but do not boil the remaining ingredients. Combine with syrup, garnish with lemon slices, and serve hot. Makes twenty servings.

—The Williamsburg Cookbook

1 cup sugar
4 cinnamon sticks
lemon slices
2 cups pineapple juice
2 cups orange juice
6 cups dry red wine
½ cup lemon juice
1 cup dry sherry

Wigs

Add yeast to warm water. When dissolved, add milk. Sift flour and salt into liquid and stir until blended. Mix in egg, sugar, butter, seeds, and spices. Cover bowl, put in a warm place free from drafts, and let double in bulk. Stir down and add enough flour to make a kneadable dough. Turn out onto floured board and knead for about 5 minutes. Place in a greased bowl, cover, and let double in bulk again. Punch down and turn out onto floured board. Roll or pat to ¼- to ½-inch thickness. Cut into wedges or whatever shape is desired. Place on greased baking sheets. Cover with towel or cloth and let rise until doubled in bulk. Bake at 375° for about 20 minutes, or until lightly browned. Makes two to four dozen buns, depending on shape and thickness.

1 package dry yeast
¼ cup warm water
1½ cups warm milk
6 cups flour
1½ teaspoons salt
1 egg, beaten
¾ cup sugar
½ cup butter, softened
1 tablespoon caraway seeds
¼ teaspoon nutmeg
pinch ground cloves
pinch mace

—*Yuletide at Winterthur*

Christiana Campbell's Tavern Spoon Bread

Spoon bread, or batter bread, is a custardy corn bread served soufflé-hot from the dish, preferably earthenware, in which it is baked.

Preheat oven to 350°. Grease a 2-quart casserole.

Mix sugar and salt with cornmeal and blend well. Add butter and pour in 1⅓ cups boiling water, stirring constantly. Allow to cool.

Beat eggs with baking powder until very light and fluffy, then add to cornmeal mixture. Stir in milk and pour into prepared casserole. Place casserole in shallow pan of hot water and bake at 350° for 35 to 40 minutes. Serve hot. Makes eight servings.

1⅓ teaspoons sugar
1½ teaspoons salt
1 cup cornmeal
4 tablespoons butter
3 eggs
1 tablespoon baking powder
1⅓ cups hot milk

—*The Williamsburg Cookbook*

King's Arms Tavern
Cream of Peanut Soup

In 1794, Thomas Jefferson recorded the yield of sixty-five peanut hills at Monticello. The cultivation of peanuts increased in the South in the nineteenth century, but it was not until after the Civil War that they gained national acceptance.

Sauté onion and celery in butter until soft but not brown. Stir in flour until well blended. Add chicken stock, stirring constantly, and bring to a boil. Remove from heat and rub through a sieve. Add peanut butter and cream, stirring to blend thoroughly. Return to low heat, but do not boil, and serve, garnished with chopped peanuts. Makes ten to twelve servings.

    Note. This soup is also good served ice cold. To serve cold, use 1 tablespoon butter and 3 tablespoons peanut or vegetable oil in place of the ¼ cup butter. Thin out with additional milk if necessary.

           —The Williamsburg Cookbook

1 medium onion, chopped
2 ribs of celery, chopped
¼ cup butter
3 tablespoons all-purpose
  flour
2 quarts homemade
  chicken stock or canned
  chicken broth
2 cups smooth peanut
  butter
1¾ cups light cream
peanuts, chopped

Oyster Stew

Drain oysters and reserve liquor. Melt all but 2 teaspoons of the butter over medium heat and add salt, pepper, and Tabasco sauce. Add oyster liquor to butter and seasonings; stir to blend. Add oysters and cook only until edges begin to curl. Stir in milk and cream and bring almost to the boiling point. Serve in hot bowls, top with remaining butter, and sprinkle with paprika. Makes four servings.

           —The Williamsburg Cookbook

1 pint shucked oysters
4 tablespoons butter
¾ teaspoon salt
pepper to taste
dash Tabasco sauce
2 cups milk
2 cups light cream
paprika

Wine Jelly Mold with Custard Sauce

Soften gelatin in 1½ cups cold water for 5 minutes. Dissolve sugar in 1 quart of hot water and bring to a boil, then remove from heat. Add lemon juice, rind, and softened gelatin. Stir well and allow to stand 5 minutes, then strain mixture through cheesecloth. Add wine, stirring gently to avoid making air bubbles.

Pour slowly into 8-cup mold and chill at least 6 hours, or until firm. Unmold onto chilled serving dish. Serve with custard sauce or garnish lightly with whipped cream and red glazed cherries. Makes ten to twelve servings.

4 envelopes unflavored gelatin
2 cups sugar
6 tablespoons lemon juice
rind of 3 lemons, grated
2½ cups burgundy or any other dry red wine

Custard Sauce

Dissolve cornstarch in ¼ cup cream. In a bowl, beat egg yolks until light, then add cornstarch mixture. Heat remaining cream, taking care not to boil, and add sugar and salt. Pour over egg mixture in bowl, stirring constantly.

Pour sauce back into saucepan, return to low heat, and continue to stir and cook 5 minutes, or until slightly thickened. Add vanilla, blend thoroughly, and cool. Makes about two and a half cups.

1½ tablespoons cornstarch
2 cups light cream, divided
4 egg yolks
½ cup sugar
pinch salt
1 teaspoon vanilla

—*The Williamsburg Cookbook*

Virginia Ham and Brandied Peaches

Williamsburg visitors who carry home a Virginia ham are advised to heed these preliminary directions or they may be sadly disappointed:

Scrub the ham to remove the coating of seasonings; cover it with water and soak for 24 hours. Place the ham, skin side down, in a pan with enough fresh water to cover; bring to a boil, then reduce heat and simmer, covered, for 20 to 25 minutes per pound. When done, skin the ham and trim off excess fat.

Note. These directions apply to a Virginia ham that has been cured for at least 12 months.

If the ham has been cured less than 12 months, follow instructions on the wrapper or hang the ham and allow it to age.

Preheat oven to 375°. Combine brown sugar, bread crumbs, and cloves and press mixture into the ham. Place the ham in a shallow baking pan and bake at 375° for 15 minutes, or until sugar melts. Remove from oven and drizzle honey, sherry, or sweet-pickle vinegar on the ham. Return to the oven for 15 minutes. Serve garnished with brandied peaches, spiced crab apples, or any other spiced fruit.

Virginia ham (10 to 12 pounds)
2 tablespoons light brown sugar
1 tablespoon bread crumbs
1 teaspoon ground cloves
3 tablespoons honey, dry sherry, or sweet-pickle vinegar

Brandied Peaches

Sent to family or friends back home in England, a Virginia ham made a delectable and much appreciated gift. So did peach brandy. In a letter of 1758 to Theodorick Bland, Sr., of Virginia, the Liverpool merchant Charles Gore expressed his thanks for the "kind present of hams and peach brandy."

Another favorite was brandied peaches. St. George Tucker of Williamsburg, writing to his daughter in 1804, passed on a recipe for "Brandy Peaches."

Brandied peaches can now be prepared by a quick method, providing an excellent accompaniment to Virginia ham.

Drain the peaches and reserve 1 cup of the juice. Mix the sugar with the reserved peach juice and boil until reduced to one-half the original quantity. Cool, measure, and stir in the brandy and the almond extract. Pour brandy syrup over peaches and serve, or pack peaches in a sterilized one-quart glass jar, add the brandy syrup, and seal. Makes about one quart.

2 cans (1 pound, 13 ounces each) peach halves
1 cup sugar
½ cup brandy, preferably a peach or other fruit brandy
3 to 4 drops almond extract

—*The Williamsburg Cookbook*

Chicken Pie

Place chicken pieces, onion, carrots, and celery in a large saucepan or pot. Add six cups water, season with salt and pepper, and bring to a boil. Lower heat to a simmer and cook until chicken is tender (no more than ½ hour). When chicken is done, place a colander over another pot, or a large bowl, and strain out chicken and vegetables. Return broth to pot, and continue to simmer over very low heat.

When chicken is cool enough to handle, remove skin and bones and add these to the broth. Cut chicken meat into 1-inch chunks and place them and the carrots and celery in a covered bowl (discard onion, or return to broth in pot). Raise heat under broth and reduce to about 3 cups. Strain, and keep hot.

Melt butter or chicken fat in a heavy saucepan. Add flour and stir well. Cook for 2 minutes, then add hot broth all at once. Whisk or stir vigorously until smooth. Lower heat and, stirring from time to time, simmer for 15 minutes. Then pour this thickened broth over the chicken chunks and vegetables. Mix well, and let cool to room temperature. Taste, and adjust seasoning.

Line the bottom of a 9-inch shallow ovenproof casserole with pastry, allowing a 1-inch overhang around the rim. Add the cooled chicken mixture. Moisten the overhanging pastry with a little cold water or milk, cover the top with pastry rolled out to a 10-inch circle, press edges together to seal well, trim, and crimp decoratively. Cut a few slashes in top crust, place casserole onto a large baking tin, and bake in a 400° oven until top is golden brown. Makes six to eight servings.

Note. To glaze crust, brush with 1 egg yolk mixed with 1 tablespoon milk or cream. For an extra-shiny crust, brush top again after the pie has baked for 15 minutes. The pie may also be baked with a top crust only.

—Adapted from *Yuletide at Winterthur*

2 four-pound chickens, quartered
1 large onion, quartered
3 carrots, scraped and cut into ½-inch chunks
4 stalks celery, sliced into ½-inch pieces
salt and pepper
2 tablespoons butter or chicken fat
3 tablespoons flour
pastry for top and bottom crust

Roast Suckling Pig

Obtain a dressed suckling pig of about 10 to 12 pounds. (A suckling pig of this size is 20–24 inches in length and requires a wide oven and a large pan.) Allow 1¼ pounds uncooked weight per person. Stuff the pig with a traditional fruit or sausage stuffing, allowing 1 cup dressing per pound. Sew up the pig and use a small block of wood or crumpled ball of aluminum foil to keep its mouth open. Rub the pig all over with a mixture of oil and flour. Cover tail and ears with foil. Brown at 450° for 15 minutes, reduce heat to 325°, and roast until tender, about 25 to 30 minutes per pound. Baste often. Remove pig from oven. Remove foil from tail and ears, replace block with an apple, use cranberries or small prunes for eyes, and place on platter. If possible, drape a green wreath around neck and surround with hot spiced whole fruits or stuffed tomatoes. Serve with gravy made from pan juices. Makes eight to ten servings.

—Yuletide at Winterthur

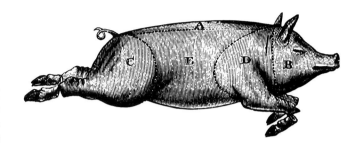

Plum Pudding

Pour milk over bread and stir. Add suet, sugar, eggs, brandy, and vanilla, and mix completely. In a larger bowl, mix raisins, currants, nuts, and orange peel. Sift flour, soda, and salt and combine with spices. Add to the fruit-and-nut mixture and blend. Combine the two mixtures and stir well.

Pour pudding into a greased 2-quart mold (do not use tube or bundt pan or ring mold). Cover the mold completely with foil, using string to secure. Put the mold on a rack within a deep pot or Dutch oven. Add boiling water to the pot to a depth of 2 inches, cover, and steam the pudding for about 3½ hours. Be sure water level is maintained in pot; if water is added, make sure it is boiling. Remove mold and cool for 15 to 20 minutes. Unmold pudding onto serving plate. Serve with wine sauce or hard sauce of your choice. Makes twelve to sixteen servings.

—Yuletide at Winterthur

1 cup milk
4 slices stale bread, cubed
6 ounces suet, ground
1 cup brown sugar, packed
2 eggs, beaten
¼ cup brandy
1 teaspoon vanilla
2 cups raisins
1 cup currants
½ cup nuts, chopped
½ cup candied orange peel
1 cup flour
1 teaspoon baking soda
½ teaspoon salt
2 teaspoons cinnamon
1 teaspoon mace
1 teaspoon ground cloves

Fruitcake

Cream butter and sugar. Add eggs, one at a time, orange juice, and vanilla. Mix in flour, baking powder, and salt. Add fruits, nuts, and peels. Let batter rest for about ½ hour. Grease 10-inch tube pan (not a bundt pan). Line both bottom and sides with waxed paper; grease and flour paper. Pour batter into pan and bake at 250° for 3 hours. Remove cake from oven and cool.

Remove cake from pan, peel off paper, and place in a covered tin lined with cheesecloth. Pour on brandy, then wrap cloth over cake. Cover and store for several days. Check cake; if too dry, add more brandy. Makes a five- to six-pound cake.

—Yuletide at Winterthur

1 cup butter
1 cup sugar
5 eggs
¼ cup orange juice
1½ teaspoons vanilla
3 cups flour, sifted
2 teaspoons baking powder
¼ teaspoon salt
1 pound raisins
1 pound candied cherries
1 pound candied pineapple
½ pound currants
½ pound citron
½ pound chopped nuts
¼ pound each, candied lemon peel and candied orange peel
1 cup brandy

Shrewsbury Cakes

Cream sugar and butter. Add egg and stir well. Sift flour and spices into creamed mixture and stir. Turn dough out onto floured board and knead a few times. Dough should be a bit crumbly. Roll dough out to ¼-inch thickness. Cut out 2-inch rounds or whatever shape you wish. Place on greased baking sheets. Bake at 350° for 10 to 12 minutes, or until bottoms of cookies are lightly browned. Makes three dozen cookies.

—Yuletide at Winterthur

½ cup sugar
½ cup butter
1 egg, beaten
2 cups flour
½ teaspoon cinnamon
¼ teaspoon nutmeg

Honey Cookies

Cream butter and sugar. Add eggs, honey, and water. Add to the flour the baking soda, cream of tartar, salt, and spices. Add flour mixture to creamed mixture. Blend thoroughly and refrigerate for about 1 hour. Roll dough about ¼ inch thick and cut into desired shapes. Bake at 350° until cookies are delicately browned. Makes four to five dozen cookies.

—Yuletide at Winterthur

1 cup butter
1 cup sugar
2 eggs
2 cups honey
⅔ cup water
7 cups flour
4 teaspoons baking soda
3 teaspoons cream of tartar
1 teaspoon salt
1 teaspoon cinnamon
1 teaspoon ginger
1 teaspoon nutmeg

Jumbles

Cream butter and sugar. Add egg and vanilla and mix completely. Blend spices with flour and add to creamed mixture. Drop from a teaspoon, 2 inches apart, onto a greased baking sheet. Bake at 350° until edges are golden brown. Optional: Before baking, top each cookie with a nut meat, raisin, or piece of citron or candied fruit. Makes about two dozen cookies.

⅓ cup sugar
½ cup butter
1 egg
1 teaspoon vanilla
1 teaspoon cinnamon
½ teaspoon nutmeg
⅔ cup flour

—*Yuletide at Winterthur*

To Candy Any Sort of Flowers

Take the best treble refined sugar, break it into lumps, and dip it piece by piece into water, put them into a vessel of silver, and melt them over the fire; when it just boils, strain it, and set it on the fire again and let it boil till it draws in hairs, which you may perceive by holding up your spoon, then put in the flowers, and set them in cups or glasses. When it is of a hard candy, break it in lumps, and lay it as high as you please. Dry it in a stove, or in the sun, and it will look like sugar-candy.

—Hannah Glasse, *The Art of Cookery*, 1805

Frosted or Candied Rose Petals

Pick just-opened roses. Dip into water to wash and pat dry. Separate the petals. One at a time, dip into egg whites beaten with a small amount of water. Coat each petal with superfine sugar either by dusting from a shaker or by "painting" with a cotton swab or small, fine artist's brush. Place finished petals on baking sheet; do not overlap. Put in 200° oven until completely dry. Place in an airtight container, separating layers of petals with waxed paper. Store in a dry, cool place.

Note. Make sure roses have not been sprayed or dusted with pesticides for at least a week prior to picking. They should be picked early in the morning, preferably while still bedewed and before the sun has touched them. The best roses for candying are old-fashioned tea roses with a heavy, strong fragrance. If a stronger rose flavor is desired, substitute rosewater for the water added to the egg whites.

—*Yuletide at Winterthur*

VICTORIAN AMERICA

In the entrance hall of the Mark Twain house, a simple arrangement of greens adds a holiday note to the splendid mantel flanked by bronze reproductions of famous statues in Paris and Tiffany wall stenciling.
Photograph by Spencer A. Sloan

CELEBRATES 1850–1910

The Mark Twain House

Samuel Clemens, better known as Mark Twain, was wont to complain about the hectic holiday pace—the "infernal" entertaining and shopping—and he always waited until the last minute before joining in the festivities. However, despite his disparaging comments, it was he who dressed as Santa for the children and playfully ran around pretending to warm himself after his long drive in the snow. And once he signed a letter to his daughter Susy, "Your loving Santa Claus, Palace of St. Nicholas in the Moon."

Mrs. Clemens had a "secret wrapping room" for the mounds of presents that would go under the Christmas tree. On Christmas Day, Twain and the Clemens girls delivered by sleigh the gifts for friends, and for the poor, that Mrs. Clemens had carefully prepared.

Twain's Hartford, Connecticut, house, built in 1874 at the height of his prosperity, reflects his extravagant hospitality and unique exuberance. The magnificent dining room, decorated by the Louis Comfort Tiffany Studios, is the perfect setting for a grand and lively Christmas feast. Each holiday season the house is decked with greenery just as it was when the Clemenses lived there with their three daughters, and throngs of visitors come to enjoy the spirit of a Clemens family Christmas.

Opposite: *Mountains of presents were always found under the Clemens's Christmas tree, except the year when the "huge black thing" seen secretly by the children in the dark of night turned out on Christmas morning to be a piano.*
Photograph by Spencer A. Sloan

Above (right): *Even the parlor chandelier is draped with greens and ribbons in the Mark Twain house.*
Photograph by Spencer A. Sloan

Right: *The stairwell, with evergreen garlands wrapped around the banister and looped through the balusters (all the way to the third floor) and a big red bow tied on the newel post, is decorated in the Clemens family's own style.*
Photograph by Spencer A. Sloan

Below: *On the Victorian Christmas dinner table it was not unusual for the last rosebuds of fall, preserved by a method that began with dipping the stem ends in melted paraffin, to bloom afresh.*
Photograph by Spencer A. Sloan

VERY VICTORIAN CHRISTMASES

The degree to which Christmas was celebrated in the early years of American history varied enormously from one family to another even within the same geographical region. The presence or absence of gifts and a gift-bringer (and his identity, appearance, and timing), and the inclusion or omission of a Christmas tree—these basic aspects of the modern Yuletide were not standardized until well after 1840.

Even in areas settled largely by Anglicans, where Christmas was widely accepted, the old English-style Yuletide that Washington Irving had so appealingly romanticized had not always been wholeheartedly applauded. As hostilities with the mother country crescendoed in the War of 1812, it became well-nigh unpatriotic in some quarters to celebrate Christmas in the English fashion. Possibly it was for that reason that Britain's Yule log, which the Virginia planters enjoyed, never became as popular as a handful of other customs that were primarily the legacy of other immigrant groups.

Be that as it may, by the time Victoria ascended the throne, the Christmas customs brought to these shores from Europe had mingled and melded, and America was well on its way to developing a set of Christmas customs all its own.

When Victoria married Albert, a German, in 1840 and decked out a small royal tree that was pictured in ladies' magazines on both sides of the Atlantic, the Christmas tree became as fashionable for adults as it had been delightful for children.

In America during the Christmas season the community at large buzzed with special events: concerts, exhibitions, masquerade balls, shooting matches, turkey hunts, and billiard tournaments. Taffy pulls and skating, sledding, and sleighing parties were common. Victorian holiday makers flocked to special Christmas fairs, eager to see the community Christmas tree or Nativity scene and hoping to win a door prize—a piano, sewing machine, set of parlor furniture, or other useful item.

Housewives began their holiday planning weeks in advance, preparing sweets to make callers welcome or to cheer the lonely widow down the road. Houses were decorated with greens, and Christmas trees set up. The tradition of the Christmas tree came into its own during the nineteenth century. Newspapers and magazines had reported on the trees that had appeared earlier in Philadelphia and Rochester and Wooster (Ohio) and Cleveland and Richmond. Readers became curious . . . entrepreneurs set up trees and charged admission . . . rural youths took to inviting their best girls to town to view these curiosities . . . the press duly described the crowds and the

"extraordinary" object they had come to see . . . neighbors, one by one, tried dressing their own . . . and thus the custom spread.

By 1847, home trees had become so common, at least in some areas, that the editors of the second edition of *Kriss Kringle's Christmas Tree* noted that they were superseding stockings hung in the chimney corner as repositories for Kriss Kringle's toys, books, and bonbons. Trees began to appear at the nation's Sun-

day schools' holiday celebrations at about this time, and though not without their critics, they were a high point of the year for youngsters, particularly those who did not have trees at home. By 1848, the Philadelphia *Pennsylvanian* was reporting that the city's markets were "almost impassable" as a result of the Christmas tree trade. The *Lutheran Observer* for January 2, 1863, noted a veritable forest of evergreens in the public square and along the streets of Lancaster. And in New York City the trees destined for local homes, some two hundred thousand of them, brought from all over the Northeast, were piled so high along the sidewalk that merchants were obliged to keep their gaslights on even during daylight hours.

In New York hundreds of advertisements touting the suitability of certain items as Christmas gifts appeared in local papers. It was in a New York paper, *The Sun*, that editor Francis P. Church declared, in answering a letter from a doubting young Victorian, "Yes, Virginia, there is a Santa Claus."

Meanwhile, the December 25, 1852, edition of *Gleason's Pictorial* numbered Christmas trees "among the household gods" of New England and elsewhere. Newspapers like the Philadelphia *Weekly Press* noted in 1877 that Americans might as well "dance without music, or attempt to write a poem without rhythm," as to keep Christmas without a Christmas tree.

Decorating the Tree

The Christmas trees that Prince Albert and his countrymen set up were usually small enough to stand on a tabletop. In America, however, trees began reaching a height of seven, eight, nine, or even more feet to accommodate the wealth of ready-made Christmas tree ornaments that were increasingly available.

There were always candles—generally attached by clip-on holders. But the ingenuity of American inventors was nearly inexhaustible, and in the days before electric lights families had their choice of innumerable other types of lighting devices, including miniature oil lamps and tin lanterns with isinglass windows.

From confectioners there were great necklaces of unwrapped hard candies in rainbow hues, preserved coriander seeds, chocolates encased in gold

Above: *The Christmas tree in the library, where the Clemens family gathered in the afternoon for storytelling.*
Photograph by Spencer A. Sloan

Opposite (above): *The Clemens family on the "Ombra" of their Hartford residence, about 1884.*
Courtesy The Bancroft Library

Opposite (below): *Mark Twain's Hartford house, in which he lived with his family from 1874 to 1891.*
Courtesy Mark Twain Memorial

Text continued on page 64

Above: *The Clemens dining room ready for Christmas dinner. Although Mark Twain complained that banquets were "probably the most fatiguing thing in the world except ditchdigging," an open-house policy prevailed in his elegant Victorian residence, and the frequent guests were luxuriously wined and dined.*
Photograph by Spencer A. Sloan

Christmas Dinner with Mark Twain *is based on an 1887 banquet menu from Mark Twain's Hartford residence and an 1870s Christmas dinner from the Butler-McCook Homestead, also in Hartford. Both menus and the recipes that follow (except for the Sweet Mince Cake and the Spanish Cream, which are from the Hartford Mark Twain Memorial) are from* Connecticut à la Carte © 1982.

Christmas Dinner With Mark Twain

Romaine Punch

Champagne   Claret Wine

Tomato Aspic and Dressing

Chestnut Soup   Champignons Flambés

Cranberry Relish

Sweetbreads in Port Wine Sauce

Roast Turkey with Warwick Maize Sausage Stuffing

Pheasant Cumberland

New Potatoes in Savory Sauce   Soused Gourmet Onions

Toffee Bars   Chocolate Truffles   Pumpkin Pecan Pie

Christmas Pudding with Caramel Sauce

Mark Twain's Favorite Sweet Mince Cake   Mark Twain's Spanish Cream

Coffee in the Drawing Room

Romaine Punch

This punch was served at Mark Twain's Hartford house in 1887. It was also served by President and Mrs. Grant at an elaborate breakfast in the State Dining Room after the marriage of their daughter, Nellie.

Combine water and sugar; stir until sugar dissolves. Stir in lemon juice. Freeze at least 3 hours. Remove from freezer about 1 hour before serving; thaw mixture to slush. Divide mixture evenly among 4 glasses. Combine brandy and rum; pour 1 jigger (1½ ounces) of the mixture into each glass. Stir well to mix. Freeze until served.

1⅔ cups cold water
⅓ cup sugar
⅓ cup lemon juice
2 jiggers (3 ounces) brandy
2 jiggers (3 ounces) light rum

Tomato Aspic and Dressing

Simmer first four ingredients 10 minutes; strain and pour mixture over lemon gelatin. Add vinegar and unflavored gelatin. Pour into a greased 1-quart mold and chill until set.

3½ cups tomato juice
½ teaspoon celery salt
1 tablespoon grated onion
6 whole cloves
1 box (6 ounces) lemon gelatin
2 tablespoons vinegar (1 tablespoon white, 1 tablespoon wine)
1 envelope unflavored gelatin

Sour Cream Horseradish Dressing

Combine dressing ingredients to taste and chill overnight. Unmold aspic on decorative platter; accompany with dressing in small bowl. Makes four cups aspic.

    Note. Recipe doubles or triples easily. Mold can be made several days ahead. If using a ring mold, fill center with fresh shrimp and surround with sliced avocado.

½ cup sour cream or crème fraîche
½ cup commercial or homemade mayonnaise
horseradish to taste
¼ cup thinly sliced scallions, white and green parts

Chestnut Soup

In a large saucepan, sauté celery, carrot, and onion in butter until tender. Add chicken stock, parsley, bay leaf, and clove; bring to boil; simmer 15 minutes.

Purée chestnuts, add to stock; add Madeira, simmer 3 minutes. Remove parsley, bay leaf, and clove; put contents of pan in blender or food processor; purée. Return to pan, add cream; stir over moderate heat until hot, but do not let boil. Add salt and pepper to taste. Add more Madeira, if desired, and serve. Makes eight to ten servings.

¼ cup chopped celery
¼ cup chopped carrot
¼ cup chopped onion
2 tablespoons butter
4 cups chicken stock
2 sprigs parsley
1 bay leaf
1 clove
1 cup fresh cooked
    chestnuts or 1 can
    (1 pound) chestnuts,
    drained
¼–½ cup Madeira wine or
    sherry
½ cup cream
salt
freshly ground pepper

Champignons Flambés
(Flamed Mushrooms)

Remove stems from mushrooms and save for soup. Melt butter in a skillet and sauté mushrooms. Season with salt, pepper, and tarragon.

Heat cognac in small pan. As soon as mushrooms begin to brown, pour cognac over them and flame. When flame has died down, spoon liquid over mushrooms; cook 2 minutes more; serve. Makes six servings.

1½ pounds mushrooms
5 tablespoons butter
½ teaspoon salt
freshly ground pepper
1 teaspoon crushed
    tarragon
½ cup cognac

Uncooked Fresh Cranberry Relish

Grind cranberries, apple, orange, and fennel with coarse blade of food grinder or in food processor. Add marmalade, honey, and walnuts; stir until well mixed. Refrigerate until serving time. Makes ten servings.

1 pound fresh cranberries,
    washed
1 apple, cored and
    quartered
1 orange, washed,
    quartered, and seeded
1 fennel bulb, including 3
    stalks, cut up
6 tablespoons orange or
    tangerine marmalade
3 tablespoons honey
½ cup chopped walnuts

Sweetbreads in Port Wine Sauce

Sweetbreads were among Mark Twain's favorite delicacies. It is possible that his recipe was from The Housekeeper and Healthkeeper, *written in 1873 by Catherine E. Beecher, a sister of Harriet Beecher Stowe, and Mark Twain's friend and nearest neighbor. The recipe reads: "The best way to cook sweetbreads is to broil them thus: Parboil them, and then put them on a clean gridiron for broiling. When delicately browned, take them off and roll in melted butter on a plate, to prevent their being dry and hard. Some cook them on a griddle well buttered, turning frequently; and some put narrow strips of salt pork on them while cooking."*

Soak sweetbreads for 1 hour in cold water. Drain. Put into saucepan with cold water and lemon juice; bring slowly to a boil and simmer 10 minutes. Drain, put into a bowl of ice water for 15 minutes or until ready to use. Remove skin and sinews and dry. Season with salt and pepper; dust with flour. Brown sweetbreads on both sides in butter over moderate heat. Remove and keep warm while preparing sauce.

2 pairs large sweetbreads
1 tablespoon lemon juice
salt
freshly ground pepper
2 tablespoons flour
2 tablespoons butter

Port Wine Sauce

In 2-quart saucepan, reduce port wine and orange juice to syrupy glaze. Add chicken stock and boil until reduced by half. While sauce is still boiling hard, add the cream; do not stir. Boil vigorously 5 minutes or until surface is full of small, tight bubbles. Then stir gently until sauce is thick enough to coat spoon. Remove from heat. Season to taste with salt and pepper.

For each serving, arrange half a sweetbread on a hot plate and nap with ¼ cup sauce. Makes four servings.

Note. Calf's liver, 1¼ pounds cut into 4 slices ⅓-inch thick, or an equal amount of chicken livers, can be used instead of sweetbreads.

1 cup ruby port
juice of 1 orange
1⅓ cups chicken stock
⅓ cup heavy cream
salt
freshly ground pepper

Roast Turkey in Paper Bag with Warwick Maize Sausage Stuffing

This method for roasting turkey is foolproof! The bird emerges extremely moist, a beautiful rich golden brown—with absolutely no watching, basting, or worrying.

Turkey Stock

Simmer turkey neck and giblets in water with celery, onion, carrot, salt, and pepper for 3 hours. Strain, and reserve giblets. (Turkey stock may be made a day in advance).

turkey neck and giblets
4 cups water
2 stalks celery, chopped
1 large onion, chopped
1 large carrot, chopped
salt
freshly ground pepper

Warwick Maize Sausage Stuffing

Crumble bread and corn bread in large bowl; combine with parsley, sage, marjoram, thyme, salt, and pepper. Set aside.

Sauté crumbled sausage in a large, heavy skillet. Drain on paper towels; add to cornbread mixture. Add butter to sausage drippings and sauté onion and liver for 10 minutes. Add celery, cook 5 minutes more. Transfer to cornbread mixture, add oysters to skillet and cook until the edges curl. Remove and add to dressing. Combine dressing with enough turkey stock (⅓ to ½ cup) to moisten.

2 cups toasted bread cubes
6 cups day-old corn bread
¼ cup minced parsley
3 tablespoons sage
1 teaspoon marjoram
1 teaspoon thyme
1 tablespoon salt
1 teaspoon pepper
½ pound hot bulk sausage,
*   crumbled*
4 tablespoons butter
1½ cups chopped onion
turkey liver, chopped
1 cup finely chopped celery
1 pint fresh shucked oysters

Roast Turkey

Stuff and truss turkey. Place ½ pound butter, broken into small pieces, in the bottom of brown paper bag. (Be certain the seam side of bag is on the top, not the bottom, where you are placing butter.) Rub outside of turkey thoroughly with remaining butter. Seal bag by stapling open end together, so that no air can get in. If sealed well, turkey will be very moist. Place bag on as high a rack as possible in roasting pan containing 1½ inches of water. Roast turkey in preheated 325° oven for 3½ hours. When time

1 12–15-pound turkey
1 pound butter
large brown paper bag

is up, slit open bottom of bag while still in oven, so that all juices will drain into roasting pan; check for doneness with meat thermometer. If not done, finish roasting turkey in conventional manner. When done, remove from oven and let rest 20 to 30 minutes. Make gravy while turkey rests.

Turkey Gravy

Pour fat and meat juices from roasting pan into bowl, leaving all brown bits in pan. Let fat rise to top of bowl; skim it off, but reserve in another bowl. For each cup of gravy desired, measure 1 tablespoon fat and put back in roasting pan. Set over low heat. Measure 1 tablespoon flour for each cup gravy. Blend flour into fat in pan. Cook until bubbly, stirring constantly. Brown flour to obtain more color for gravy. You will need 1 cup liquid for each cup of finished gravy. Use reserved pan juices and turkey stock. If extra liquid is needed, use canned chicken stock. Add lukewarm stock to flour mixture all at once. Cook, stirring constantly, until thickened, scraping up all brown bits. Add chopped cooked giblets, if desired. Season to taste.

fat
flour
pan juices
turkey stock

Pheasant Cumberland

Roast Pheasant with Red Cabbage Garnish

Place bacon and butter in low, heavy, ovenproof casserole. Melt butter; add onion and carrot and cook gently 3 to 4 minutes. Remove bacon and reserve. Raise heat and brown pheasants. Remove birds to heated platter. Add spices, salt, brandy, wine to casserole; simmer 3 minutes.

Meanwhile, secure the strips of bacon across breasts of pheasants with toothpicks. Return birds, breast side up, to casserole; surround them with whole apples and onions. Roast in preheated 300° oven 1¼ hours, basting birds, apples, and onions frequently. Remove birds and arrange attractively on top of Red Cabbage Garnish, along with apples and onions. Pour pan juices over birds. Makes four to six servings.

Note. Two large Cornish Game Hens (two pounds each) can be used if pheasant is not available.

6 slices lean bacon
4 tablespoons butter
1 small onion, finely chopped
¼ cup finely chopped carrot
2 pheasants
¼ teaspoon ground mace
¼ teaspoon cayenne pepper
salt
¼ cup brandy
½ cup port, sherry, or red wine
4 medium apples (Golden Delicious), peeled and cored but left whole
8–12 small onions, peeled

Red Cabbage Garnish

Melt butter and gently sauté onion for 3 to 4 minutes. Stir in apple slices, then all remaining ingredients. Season to taste; if necessary, add a few tablespoons water. Cover tightly and simmer 20 to 25 minutes. Check before serving to see if more salt should be added. Makes four to six servings.

6 tablespoons butter
1 large onion, finely sliced
1 large green apple, peeled, cored, and sliced
½ red cabbage, shredded
1 tablespoon lemon juice
salt
freshly ground pepper
½ teaspoon thyme
2 tablespoons chopped parsley
water as needed

New Potatoes in Savory Sauce

In 4-quart saucepan, place potatoes in salted water to cover. Bring to boil over medium heat, cook gently 15 to 20 minutes, until fork tender. Drain. Peel potatoes or leave skins on. Keep warm.

Heat butter and oil. Stir in rind, parsley, chives, nutmeg, flour, salt, and pepper. Heat slowly while stirring. Do not boil. Sauce will thicken slightly. (Up to this point, may be made earlier in day; keep at room temperature until serving.) At serving time, stir lemon juice into warmed sauce. Pour mixture over potatoes. Toss to coat. Makes four to six servings.

2 pounds small new potatoes, unpeeled
¼ cup butter
1 tablespoon olive oil
grated rind of 1 lemon
¼ cup chopped fresh parsley or dill
2 tablespoons snipped chives
⅛ teaspoon freshly grated nutmeg
¼ teaspoon flour
¼ teaspoon salt
¼ teaspoon freshly ground pepper
3 tablespoons lemon juice

Soused Gourmet Onions

Sprinkle onions with sugar, salt, and pepper. In skillet sauté onions in melted butter 5 to 8 minutes, separating into rings. Add sherry; cover and cook 2 to 3 minutes, or until tender. Sprinkle with cheese. Serve immediately. Makes four servings.

5 medium onions, thinly sliced
½ teaspoon sugar
½ teaspoon salt
½ teaspoon freshly ground pepper
⅓ cup butter, melted
½ cup sherry
2 tablespoons freshly grated Parmesan cheese

Toffee Bars

Toffee is a generic name for many kinds of hard sweetmeats made from sugar and butter; the addition of egg and flour produces a cross between a cookie and candy.

Bars

Cream butter, add sugar gradually, beating by hand or with electric mixer until light and fluffy. Add yolk, beat well. Stir in flour. Spread evenly in lightly buttered 11 × 15-inch baking pan. Place on middle rack of preheated 350° oven. Bake 15 minutes. Remove from oven.

1 cup butter, room temperature
1 cup dark brown sugar
1 egg yolk
1 cup flour

Topping

While bars are baking, melt chocolate. Pour chocolate over bars while they are still warm. Spread quickly with spatula. Sprinkle with chopped nuts. Let cool to room temperature before cutting.

7 ounces milk chocolate
1 cup chopped walnuts

Alternate Holiday Topping

Melt white chocolate and spread as above. Cool until chocolate is firm to touch. Cut into bars. Beat confectioners' sugar with egg white and cream of tartar. Tint green. Pipe "holly" leaves onto each bar. Decorate centers with cinnamon candy "berries." Makes thirty to forty-eight bars.

14 ounces white chocolate
3 cups confectioners' sugar
1 egg white
⅛ teaspoon cream of tartar
green food coloring
red cinnamon candies

Chocolate Truffles in Disguise

Pastry

In large bowl of electric mixer cream butter; add vanilla and sugar and mix until smooth. On low speed, add flour, scraping bowl with rubber spatula; beat until mixture holds together. Transfer dough to piece of waxed paper. Flatten slightly and shape into an oblong. Wrap airtight; refrigerate briefly while preparing truffles.

1 cup (½ pound) butter, softened
½ teaspoon vanilla extract
½ cup confectioners' sugar
2 cups sifted flour

Truffles

Combine ground chocolate and almonds in food processor or bowl. Mix in unbeaten egg whites; knead until mixture holds together. Divide into 40 pieces, using 1 tablespoon for each, placing on waxed paper.

Remove pastry from refrigerator; it should not be chilled hard. Cut into 40 pieces. Flatten a piece in palm of hand and wrap around truffle completely. Roll into ball between palms. (Dust hands with confectioners' sugar if dough sticks.) Place on ungreased baking sheets 1 inch apart.

Bake on rack ⅓ down from top of preheated 375° oven 18 to 20 minutes, or until lightly colored. Reverse position of baking sheet if necessary during baking to ensure even browning. Cool on baking sheets a minute or two; then with wide metal spatula transfer to rack to cool. Optional: Top cooled cookies with a sifting of confectioners' sugar. Makes forty cookies.

8 ounces (½ pound) sweet chocolate very finely ground (cut coarsely, then add to food processor)
8 ounces (½ pound, or 1⅔ cups) almonds (blanched or not), very finely ground
2 egg whites, jumbo or extra-large
confectioners' sugar

Pumpkin Pecan Pie

In medium bowl, combine eggs with pumpkin, corn syrup, sugar, cinnamon, and salt. Pour into pie shell. Sprinkle with pecans. Place on middle rack of preheated 350° oven. Bake 50 to 60 minutes, until knife inserted in center comes out clean. Remove from oven; let cool on rack to room temperature. Refrigerate several hours to chill.

3 eggs, beaten until frothy
1½ cups puréed cooked or canned pumpkin
¾ cup dark corn syrup
¾ cup sugar
½ teaspoon cinnamon
¼ teaspoon salt
1 9-inch unbaked pie shell
1 cup chopped pecans

Topping

Whip cream until soft peaks form. Gradually add sugar, whipping until stiff peaks form. Spread over chilled pie. Makes six to eight servings.

1 cup heavy cream
2 tablespoons sugar

Christmas Pudding
with Caramel Sauce

Mix baking soda with carrots and potatoes. Set aside. Cream butter and sugar together; sift flour and spices over mixture; add raisins and carrot-and-potato mixture. Blend well. Place in buttered 5-cup ovenproof mold. Place mold in larger baking pan, and pour enough hot water into pan to come halfway up sides of mold. Place pan on middle rack of preheated 350° oven. Bake 60 minutes, or until pudding is set but still moist and begins to leave sides of mold. Remove pan from oven. Set mold on rack to cool. When still warm, unmold onto serving plate. (If plate is ovenproof, pudding can be re-warmed briefly in 300° oven.) Makes ten servings.

1 teaspoon baking soda
1 cup raw, finely grated carrots
1 cup raw, finely grated potatoes
½ cup butter, softened
1 cup sugar
1 cup flour
1 teaspoon cinnamon
1 teaspoon freshly grated nutmeg
1 teaspoon ground cloves
1 cup raisins, rinsed in hot water and drained

Caramel Sauce

Melt sugar and butter in top of double boiler over low heat. Add cream slowly, stirring well. Remove pan from heat. Stir in vanilla. Pass warm sauce separately or pour over pudding.

    Note. Pudding and sauce can be prepared a day ahead. Rewarm sauce gently over low heat. Unmolded pudding can be frozen for 1 month, wrapped in foil. Defrost while still wrapped. Bring to room temperature, then rewarm in 300° oven. Sprinkle pudding with whisky or brandy if dry. Pudding and sauce can be doubled successfully.

1 cup brown sugar
½ cup butter
1 cup heavy cream
1 teaspoon vanilla extract

Mark Twain's Favorite Sweet
Mince Cake

Cream butter and sugar. Add the eggs, one at a time, and beat well after each addition. Sift dry ingredients. Combine brandy and cream. Add the dry mixture and the brandy mixture alternately to the butter and sugar, beginning and ending with the dry ingredients.

    In a small bowl mix mincemeat with the two tablespoons of flour until mincemeat is well separated and covered with flour. Fold it into the batter and spoon into 9-inch tube pan that has been greased and lined with waxed paper. Bake at 325° for 1 hour and 20 minutes, until cake is golden brown and springs back when touched lightly. Cool in pan 10 minutes. Turn

1 cup butter, softened
1 cup sugar
4 eggs
2 cups sifted all-purpose flour
1 teaspoon nutmeg
½ teaspoon salt
½ teaspoon baking powder
¼ cup brandy
¼ cup heavy cream
1 9-ounce package condensed mincemeat, crumbled
2 tablespoons flour

out and serve cool. Tastes even better when toasted. Makes a four- to five-pound cake.

Mark Twain's Spanish Cream

Place milk in a 2-quart enamel or stainless steel saucepan. Sprinkle in the gelatine, and let it soften for 5 minutes. Place pan over low heat and, stirring from time to time, let milk come to scalding. In a large bowl beat egg yolks and 1 cup of sugar until thick and lemon-colored. Slowly beat in the scalded milk and mix well. Pour the mixture back into saucepan and stir constantly over low heat until it coats the spoon. Do not let it boil or it will curdle. Remove from fire and stir for 2 minutes.

In a clean bowl beat the egg whites until they stand in soft peaks, then beat in remaining cup of sugar. Fold into custard mixture, then add the wine, folding gently until all elements are well blended. Pour into a 2-quart mold that has been lightly oiled. Chill for at least 6 hours or overnight. When well set, unmold onto a serving plate. Makes ten servings.

1 quart milk
4 envelopes (1 ounce)
*   unflavored gelatine*
4 eggs, separated
2 cups sugar
1 cup wine (Madeira or
*   sherry)*

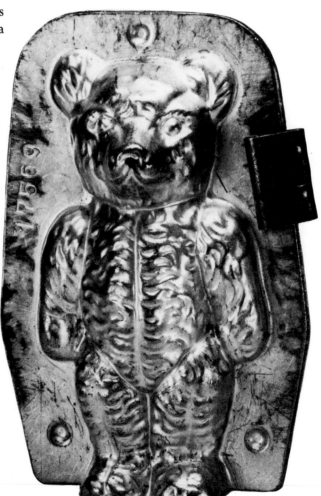

Teddy-bear candy mold. Courtesy Margaret Woodbury Strong Museum

foil, red-and-white candy sticks, and Brazil nuts (then available only during the holiday period) to suspend from a string or to stuff into cornucopias, a favorite Victorian ornament.

Imports from Germany took on increasing importance. At first these included mainly crystal icicles and rather heavy glass balls; other ornaments were made of tin in geometric shapes, sometimes studded with a "jewel" of cut glass, which, like the metal itself, would be faceted so as to glitter in the light of the candles. Later, inventions multiplied: long strings of glass beads; wax angels with wings of spun glass; gelatined candy in the shapes of trumpets and cannons, vases and acorns, and the like; tiny rolling pins and other kitchen miniatures made of wood. Embossed cardboard ornaments came in a huge variety and range. The repertory included not only simple geometric shapes, but objects such as slippers, drums, skates and sleds, and animals such as circus horses, polar bears, camels, storks, eagles, and peacocks. Even ocean liners with portholes and smokestacks and coaches and carriages detailed right down to the coachman's foot warmer were within the artists' capacity.

Elaborate versions of the cornucopias that early tree trimmers had been making out of paper were widely advertised. Candy boxes in silk and satin appeared. In 1878, Nuremburgers began to delight Americans by producing icicles made of silver foil. And the spun-glass strands called angel's hair, when pulled apart, could make the tree look as if it had been out in a blizzard.

Toys from the Victorian period. Courtesy Margaret Woodbury Strong Museum *(top) and* Smithsonian Institution *(center, bottom)*

Facsimile Victorian tree ornaments using chromolithographic prints: cotton-batting Santa Claus and cornucopias.
Photographs by Bob Hanson

In the 1890s the newly invented chromolithography process was used to produce Nativity scenes, cherubs, angels, Santa Clauses, and other holiday figures; these were printed on heavy stock, then embossed and die-cut. Intriguing butterflies, rosettes, and stars were made of crimped wire twisted and tied into shape. Papier-mâché was molded into hollow fish that could hold small candies. For the top of the tree, there were tin stars, wax-headed angels, and blown-glass "spikes" made up of a series of glass balls graduated in size, each with a concave reflecting surface. Sometimes a wax angel was suspended just above the tree so that it appeared to fly as it rotated this way and that in the currents of warm air rising from the candles.

Most delightful of all were the baubles made of blown glass. At first the German glassblowers produced only spheres, but as the artisans' skills developed, shoppers had a world of exquisite and fragile glass creations to choose among: birds, dogs, harps and trumpets, Santa Claus figures, cuckoo clocks, toadstools, teapots, houses and churches, bells that actually rang, balloons and zeppelins, yachts and steamboats, and more. The glassblowers dipped some spheres into glue and sprinkled them with crushed glass, wrapped some with nets of crinkly wire; to others they added cotton batting or chromolithographed angels or other figures. Some were lacquered by hand.

To realize why the Victorian Christmas tree evoked such wonder in its viewers one has to remember that all these trinkets in glass, tin, lead, wood, and cardboard—acquired one at a time and treasured for years—were put on the tree not instead of but usually in addition to all the traditional edible ornaments and homemade trimmings.

On Christmas Day

For children, the fact that it was on or under the Christmas tree that Santa Claus left their presents made the tree all the more enchanting. When they bounded out of bed at the crack of dawn on Christmas morning to see what treasures awaited them, it was to the Christmas tree that they raced. Sometimes the packages were opened then and there; sometimes this ritual was postponed until after

Text continued on page 70

Chateau-sur-Mer

Chateau-sur-Mer was built in Newport in 1851–52 for William S. Wetmore, who made his fortune in the China trade. At Christmas time, the Preservation Society of Newport County, Rhode Island, opens the doors of this formidable granite mansion for a splendrous Victorian Christmas "at home," complete with plum pudding and music. This was the kind of festivity for which *Mrs. Beeton's Book of Household Management*, first published in 1861, provided guidance. "Amateur friends" contributing to "at home" musical entertainments, she cautioned, should choose short pieces, and "a good break should be made between each song, solo, or recitation, for conversation," since people go to these "entertainments" to meet friends and chat with them.

A magnificent residence, Chateau-sur-Mer provides the ultimate high-style setting for a Victorian holiday celebration.

Chateau-sur-Mer's ballroom readied for the holidays. The sixteen-foot live Christmas tree is decorated with handmade ornaments—paper fans, glass beads, ribbons, candies, little gifts, and candles.
Courtesy The Preservation Society of Newport County

Opposite: *The spectacular Chateau-sur-Mer staircase draped with laurel and other evergreen garlands, all grown on the grounds of the estate.*
Courtesy The Preservation Society of Newport County

Right: *Bebe doll.*
Courtesy Margaret Woodbury Strong Museum

Below: *Bisque doll.*
Courtesy Margaret Woodbury Strong Museum

Right: *Chateau-sur-Mer, one of the finest examples of Victorian architecture in America, was built in 1852 for William S. Wetmore.*
Courtesy The Preservation Society of Newport County; photograph by John Hopf

Opposite: *Bright red ribbon bows and fresh greens on the mono-grammed Irish linen tablecloth make the formidable dining room at Chateau-sur-Mer a cheerful setting.*
Courtesy The Preservation Society of Newport County

church, another important feature of the day, or even until after dinner.

There was always a Christmas dinner. Housewives brought out their best tablecloths, their finest Rose Canton china, their crystal goblets, and their freshly polished silver. The swans, bustards, and peacocks served in England during the Twelve Days of Christmas gave way in America to ham, goose, pheasant, duck, broiled salmon, and chicken or game pie—not to mention roast turkey stuffed with chestnut or oyster or cornbread dressing, a great favorite. Then there were the vegetables—from turnips, mashed potatoes, creamed onions, creamed chestnuts, and baked stuffed potatoes to beets, fried celery, and candied sweet potatoes (thanks to improved transportation, even outside the South, where they were grown). Complementing these were creamed oysters, cheese croquettes, and innumerable bowls of jellies, pickles, and such condiments as cranberry relish.

Dessert fanciers had their choice of sponge cake, fruit cake, lemon pudding, cranberry pie, and mince pie, as well as the ever-present plum pudding, a "speckled cannonball" surrounded by a shimmering halo of blue flame. "Christmas without plum pudding would seem like . . . *Hamlet* with Hamlet left out," declared a writer in the *Woman's Home Companion* of December 1910. Oranges, rare in the country's early years, became increasingly available and were often put on the table at the end of a meal (as well as being given as prized gifts to children). Afterward, wine jelly with cream was served, and then coffee—or perhaps wine—with fruit and nuts. Wassail, hot toddy, or mulled wine was usually served as well.

Dinner over, the typical Victorian family gathered around the piano for songs or assembled for recitations of poems and ballads or for charades. Or they played old-fashioned games like blindman's buff, hide-and-seek, pin-the-beard-on-Santa-Claus, puss in the corner, and hunt the slipper. Snapdragon, a game in which players reached for, and then ate, the raisins at the bottom of a bowl full of blazing brandy, was also popular. (A handful of salt thrown into the dish after all the raisins were retrieved caused the blaze to throw off an eerie bluish glow.) There was often dancing, too, if someone could be prevailed upon to play the piano—and then cordials, eggnog, or punch

Text continued on page 74

Greenfield Village

Amid snowdrifts and flickering gas street lamps, Greenfield Village, the Henry Ford birthplace in Michigan, brings to life an old-fashioned nineteenth-century family Christmas. In the kitchens, spicy sausage and cornmeal dumplings sizzle, and walnuts, cookies, and eggshells are made into colorful tree decorations. It was during the Victorian era that the Christmas tree, gaily wrapped presents, and Santa Claus became popular. Mass communication had spread the traditions of many cultures throughout America, and new industries brought manufactured toys, Christmas cards printed on steam-operated presses, and recorded music from cylinder players.

At this special season, Greenfield Village is abuzz with holiday cooking and decorating, card making, toy exhibits, and music. Village staff members in Victorian dress are busy popping corn to string on trees, making toys and confections, including the gingerbread house. All these holiday tasks are carried on in the warm, mellow light of the gas and kerosene lamps of the Victorian period.

Opposite: *Springerle cookies, popcorn balls, and gilded nuts are among the traditional decorations prepared at Greenfield Village. In Victorian times many Christmas tree ornaments were home-crafted; the making of decorations and dressing the tree were important family activities.*
Courtesy Greenfield Village

before visitors took their leave and wended their way homeward.

From then until school reopened, Victorian children were regaled with a round of holiday parties at which they danced, played games, and received small presents. At these festivities simple refreshments—cupcakes, puddings, popcorn balls, cookies—and sweets like lemon drops rounded out the day's entertainment.

Victorian Embellishments of the Christmas Theme

By the late nineteenth century, the tree, the exchange of gifts, and the Christmas dinner had been Yuletide fare for so long that they were beginning to be called old-fashioned, and Victorians, in a relentless search for novelty, began exploring variations on these themes. Magazine writers of the period let no feature of the holiday pass without comments and suggestions.

Take the Christmas tree. Attention was paid to round trees, which were placed in the middle of the room and decorated on all sides, and to corner trees, decorated only on the sides facing the room. Admiring comment was evoked by the unusual: a tree decorated in 1897, by a successful Klondike gold miner, with some $70,000's worth of gold nuggets; a tree set up in a Harrisburg, Pennsylvania, depot, decorated not only with the usual fruits and nuts but also with a veritable shower of confetti consisting of conductors' checks and ferry tickets; a tree decorated by the University of Pennsylvania's Biological School with vertebrae and an assortment of fish, worms, crabs, and birds' nests.

Unique ornaments were a sure route to an out-of-the-ordinary creation—and so *St. Nicholas*, a monthly magazine (1873–1940) beloved of children across the country, instructed its young readers to make snowflakes by snipping white tissue paper, to craft little monkeys by stringing raisins on wires and dressing them in hats and shirts of cotton cloth, to gild popcorn strands or dye them with Easter-egg colors. Youngsters learned how to mold popcorn balls and put a surprise in the center, paint small gourds, use whole cloves to outline a name on an apple, hollow out oranges and carve them into jack-o'-lanterns.

Decorating a patriotic Christmas tree as it was done in the 1870s.
Courtesy Greenfield Village

74

Left: *Christmas sausage being prepared at Greenfield Village. A family that did not yet have one of the new ovens could prepare a full holiday meal at an open hearth, using time-honored simple recipes.*
Courtesy Greenfield Village

Below: *Making marzipan and other decorations at Greenfield Village's H. J. Heinz House.*
Courtesy Greenfield Village

Small, bright-colored kites, paper butterflies with wired wings, and whole walnuts (the kernel replaced with a fortune or a new penny and the two halves of the shell tied together with a narrow ribbon bow) were other decorations that they could manage.

Addressing themselves primarily to residents of good-sized towns and cities, ladies' magazines were quick to advise their readers on departures from the familiar scheme of glass ornaments and tinsel. For the old-fashioned look, they had a variety of tree-trimming alternatives to suggest:

Doughnuts and dried apples ("snits" as they were called in Pennsylvania Dutch country)

Garlands of cranberries, popcorn, and/or raisins

Gingerbread horses and birds

Walnuts and hickory nuts painted or wrapped in gold or silver foil

Apples, plain and gilded

Blown-out eggshells embellished with decals

Bouquets of paper flowers

Cardboard ornaments: sleighs, chariots, fairies, crosses, shields, stars

Paper goldfish and cornucopias

Lemons and oranges

Pine cones and seedpods

Colored ribbon bows and bright-colored flannel rosettes

Candied pears, apricots, crab apples, greengage plums

An appealing variant was the snow tree. Everything on it was white—candles, decorations, the wrappings—except for clear glass icicles, silver balls, and silver tinsel. Cotton batting was made glittery with a sprinkling of diamond dust, and every branch was laden with this artificial snow.

A contrast to the snow tree was the tree decorated entirely in red and green. Japanese dolls and parasols and streamers of Japanese tissue perched on its branches. The red-and-green tree was lighted exclusively by red Japanese lanterns, and gifts were wrapped in red and tied with either red or green ribbon. The theme was most striking if it was extended to the decor of the whole room, with Japanese lan-

terns replacing candles and single pine branches arranged in characteristic Oriental fashion.

Festive ideas for trees did not end there. Other tastes responded to other themes:

The icicle tree (glittering with short strands of gold and silver beads, frosted silver bells, and glass icicles)

The tree full of birds (bright-colored cloth stuffed with cotton for the bodies, tissue paper for the wings) hung on strings so as to appear to be flying

The red-and-white tree (studded with red-and-white-wrapped packages, lighted with red and white candles, festooned with strands of popcorn and cranberries, and dotted with small stockings of red and white, candy canes, and red-and-white paper flowers)

The patriotic tree (decked in red, white, and blue ribbons, balls, and packages, and an abundance of American flags; sprinkled with diamond dust for added effect and with such symbols of the variety of life in America as Chinese lanterns and Negro and Indian dolls)

If there was no space for a tree, advised the *Ladies' Home Journal* designers, one had the option of suspending a fishnet or an old hammock from the ceiling, weaving greens through the holes, and putting presents, ornaments, and candles nearby.

Victorian Ingenuity in House and Hearth

Victorian writers explored other aspects of the holiday with equal thoroughness. The decor of the house was a popular theme. Half the pleasure of decking the halls, said *Cassell's Household Guide*, lay in devising new schemes and in "giving scope to one's taste and ingenuity, new ideas springing up and developing themselves as the occasion arises, till the worker finds delight in the work, and is . . . rewarded for the toil." Evergreens were always the material of choice, the magazines advised, but the sage housewife knew that new types of greens appeared in the markets every year, and that disposing them to advantage required thought.

The classic Gingerbread House (recipe and directions on pages 84–86).
Courtesy Greenfield Village

An old-fashioned Santa Claus, 1880–1900.
Colonial Williamsburg Photograph

Mistletoe was to be hung in the hall and the dining room. To use holly, which *Cassell's* called "the prince of evergreens," the artful decorator was counseled to remove the berries and string them up in bunches, arrange the greens in any fashion desired, and then add the clusters of berries for effect. (Otherwise the berries tended to disappear among the leaves.) Boxwood and myrtle were considered to be especially effective when intertwined with everlasting flowers, Christmas roses, primulas, and camellias. The combination was adaptable to such uses as outlining a wall panel with a holiday greeting in its center. Smilax, laurel, and hemlock, which stay fresh longer than most other greens, could transform various nooks into "fairy-like bowers."

Banisters, pedestals, pillars, columns, and the frames of pictures and mirrors became verdant with garlands that the Victorian housewife made herself, using sprigs of evergreen (sprayed with water to stave off dryness) bound with twine. A device to enhance a doorway—draped as a matter of course in the Victorian household with evergreen roping interspersed with bunches of holly—was a Christmas bell made entirely of holly except for the clapper, which was covered with white mistletoe berries. Stairways lent themselves to having fishnet tacked along the balustrade and then filled with holly, laurel, and cedar to create an unbroken expanse of greenery.

In the dining room, to begin with, the chains suspending the chandelier were entwined with ropes of holly. The sideboard was set off by a small evergreen tree, or a vase filled with laurel leaves, at either end. As for the dinner table, here the Victorian imagination—and ingenuity—ran riot. By planning ahead, the hostess was able to have fresh rosebuds at each place. A few of summer's last blooms were gathered months before the holiday; the ends of their stems were dipped in melted paraffin, and the blossoms were carefully wrapped in tissue paper and stored in a cool place. On Christmas Day the coated stem ends were cut off and the roses placed in a vase of warm water, to revive and bloom for one glorious day.

For the centerpiece, there was a wide realm of possibilities. Beginning around Thanksgiving, bulbs like tulips and narcissus were forced, to provide Christmas blooms. Lilies of the valley, orchids, roses, and violets were used alone or in combination with

A sleigh ride on the grounds of Greenfield Village recalls a Currier and Ives print.
The home of Wilbur and Orville Wright is also located in Greenfield Village.
Courtesy Greenfield Village

evergreens. A low Norfolk Island pine made an attractive centerpiece with narrow scarlet ribbons extending from it to each guest's plate. Another choice was a large inverted bowl blanketed with moss stuck so thickly with sprigs of holly as to appear to consist entirely of leaves, and topped by a figure of Old Father Christmas or Santa Claus. An idea that appealed to some hostesses was a mirror centered on the table, edged with a rope of hemlock studded with bunches of holly and reflecting a wreath of holly tied with scarlet ribbon suspended above it. Others fancied, especially on a white damask cloth, a central star made out of holly with the points of the star, extending almost to the rim of the table, accented with poinsettias and in the star's center a large mound of white roses.

Harper's Bazaar of December 15, 1900, suggested leaving a polished round mahogany tabletop bare for a special holiday occasion, with holly and its berries providing the decorative motif. The leaves were to be arranged in a wreath at the center and

clusters of berries placed here and there and on each napkin. Another scheme called for the hostess's snowiest tablecloth. Atop it were placed two wreaths of holly, a small circle in the middle of the table and a large circle almost at the edge of the plates. The center of the table was presided over by a white Santa Claus in a white sleigh, sprinkled with diamond dust and filled with candy. The candlesticks were of glass with plain white shades, and dishes were either white or of glass or silver. The holly and the meal itself provided the color.

An openwork cloth inspired a colorful table if placed over scarlet sateen. The centerpiece, an épergne filled with spreading holly and red carnations, was then set on a mirror wreathed with holly. The candlesticks, with red candles, were placed so as to be reflected in the mirror. Dishes filled with candied cherries, red bonbons, and green olives carried the theme further.

At some Christmas dinners the food supplied the color. An example is the red-and-green Christmas dinner outlined by Fannie Merritt Farmer in the *Woman's Home Companion* of December 1909. Along with roast goose and baked halibut, she suggested applesauce in little baskets made of hollowed-out apples, a salad made of tomatoes cut flowerwise and served with a dab of cream cheese in the center, and a green-pepper vinaigrette dressing, as well as other foods in the colors of the season.

Even more elaborate was the "Kaleidoscope Christmas Dinner" that Constance Bristol invented for the readers of the *Woman's Home Companion* of December 1910. This was planned to "begin with the glistening whiteness of December and end amidst the glitter and color of Christmas and all its emblems." On the white-damask-covered table was a centerpiece of pine branches arranged around the base of a glass bowl filled with ferns and evergreens—the whole dotted with bits of cotton batting sprinkled with diamond dust. Around the centerpiece were four glass candlesticks, their white shades edged at top and bottom with glistening cotton and fringed with crystal beads. On white place cards the guests' names were inscribed in silver.

At the commencement of the meal, olives and white cream wafers were put out in glass and silver dishes; then came pale-colored foods: a pineapple

Doll on a velocipede.
Courtesy Margaret Woodbury Strong Museum

Opposite: *A holiday bonnet in Greenfield Village's millinery shop looks tempting in the glow of a gaslight chandelier.*
Courtesy Greenfield Village

cocktail or scalloped oysters in ramekins. The soup, perhaps cream of asparagus, was presented in gold-banded plates, a large red star cut from a pimento floating on the surface of each portion. Next followed scalloped oysters in green ramekins surrounded with holly wreaths. Before the entrée, poinsettias were brought in on a silver tray and a single flower laid in front of each plate. The roast appeared on a silver salver decorated with greens, and the vegetables were abundantly garnished with parsley. Applesauce, served in individual glass dishes, was decorated with candied cherries. Salad, garnished with balls of cream cheese and red pimento stars, was offered from a glass bowl surrounded by a wreath of holly and mistletoe. The climax, the dessert course, consisted of vanilla ice cream on red plates, each portion set in a circle of tinsel and with a Santa Claus on a stick protruding from it.

Probably only a few of Mrs. Bristol's readers followed her scheme to the letter. The kaleidoscope Christmas dinner could not by any stretch of the imagination be cited as the typical Victorian holiday repast. But it does exemplify the extent to which Christmas and its symbols had taken hold in the American mind.

Text continued on page 97

Victorian pewter ice-cream molds—a lily and a cornucopia. Courtesy Margaret Woodbury Strong Museum

The colonial tradition of setting an attractive dessert table that delighted the eye and stimulated the appetite continued through the Victorian era. A Christmas tea consisted mainly of light dishes (suitable for children's parties as well), but steamed puddings were sometimes served. Popular games at children's parties were candy pulls, peanut hunts, shadows-on-the-wall, and charades. A party favor that every young guest was happy to receive was the Christmas cracker, which opens with a loud snap when pulled by two people and yields a treasure of caps, trinkets, toys, and puzzles.

    The instructions for making the Gingerbread House and the recipes for **A Christmas Tea or Children's Party,** *which have been adapted from nineteenth-century "receipt" books, were provided by the staff of Greenfield Village.*

A Christmas Tea or Children's Party

Gingerbread House

Apple Bread   Pumpkin Bread   New York Cupcakes

Apple Dumplings

Cherry Pudding   Eve's Pudding

Warm Cream Sauce

Old-fashioned Popcorn Balls

Springerle Cookies

Cookies to Hang on the Christmas Tree

Greenfield Village's Gingerbread House

Gingerbread

Batter for one 11×17-inch pan (to be repeated twice)

Prepare the templates, following the diagrams on pages 85 and 86 and the instructions under Directions for Assembling the Gingerbread House.

Brush the softened butter evenly over one 11×17-inch baking pan. A jelly-roll pan is ideal.

Sift six cups of the flour with the baking powder, cinnamon, cloves, nutmeg, cardamom, and salt into a large mixing bowl.

In a heavy 4- or 5-quart saucepan, bring honey, sugar, and butter to a boil, stirring with a large spoon until the sugar is dissolved and the butter melted. Remove pan from heat and add lemon juice and grated rind, cooling mixture to room temperature.

Beat in two cups of the flour-and-spices mixture, add egg and egg yolk, and beat in remaining flour-and-spices mixture. Knead until dough is smooth. If too loose, add rest of flour to make a stiffer dough. Spread on the baking pan, pressing out as evenly as possible. Bake in preheated 325° oven for 35 minutes, or until cake is firm and top brown. Let cool only about 5 minutes (if cake cools too long it becomes too brittle to cut). Then, using template No. 1, cut into required shape. Let gingerbread harden.

Repeat entire process twice, for templates No. 2 and No. 3.

1 tablespoon butter, softened
6¼ cups all-purpose flour
2 tablespoons double-acting baking powder
1½ teaspoons ground cinnamon
1 teaspoon ground cloves
¼ teaspoon ground nutmeg
¼ teaspoon ground cardamom
⅛ teaspoon salt
¾ cup honey
1¾ cups sugar
¼ cup butter
⅓ cup lemon juice
1 tablespoon finely grated lemon rind
1 egg
1 egg yolk

Icing

For support and decoration

In a large bowl, beat egg whites until slightly thickened. Sift the sugar in, about ½ cup at a time, beating thoroughly. A stiff icing should be formed. Place in pastry bag for use.

Note. An extra recipe of icing may be needed to fully decorate house. Do not make the extra icing until you are ready to use it, as it hardens rapidly.

2 egg whites
2½ cups confectioners' sugar
hard candies and cookies for decorating house

Directions for assembling the Gingerbread House are on the following page.

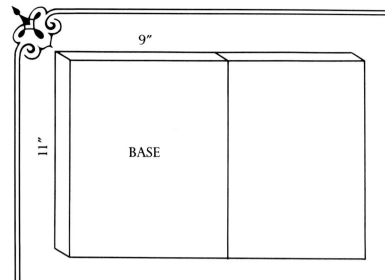

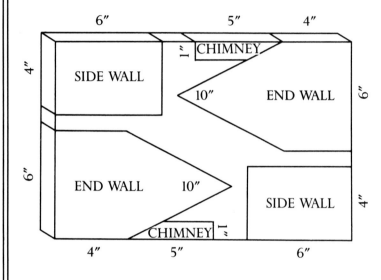

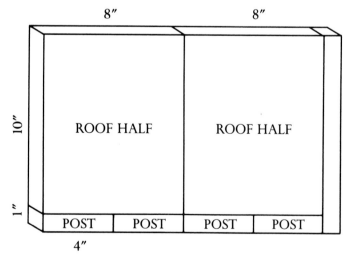

Directions for Assembling the Gingerbread House

Following the diagrams for three 11 × 17-inch sheets of gingerbread, cut out templates as designated from stiff cardboard or thin sheet metal such as tin. It is necessary to use templates in cutting out the pieces of gingerbread, rather than a freehand method, because the pieces must match exactly.

Once all the gingerbread is cut—there's plenty of scrap for "testing" the flavor, by the way—make sure the rest of the ingredients are near at hand, especially the icing. This will act as cement in construction.

Set the base piece on a cutting board or a large piece of heavy cardboard so that the house can be moved from place to place when it is finished.

Ice the bottom of one end wall—the back of the house—and the bottom and end of a side wall; fit them together and place them carefully on the base. Ice the bottom and two sides carefully. You may want to add a small support stick of gingerbread inside. Hold the pieces together until the icing has hardened. Rubber bands can be used, but be sure the gingerbread is hard enough to withstand their pressure. (See photograph.)

Repeat the procedure for the other two walls. After the walls and icing are secure, ice the top edges of the end walls and place the roof over them. The two roof pieces should meet but not overlap. Again hold or fasten in place until the icing is hardened.

You may now decorate your house as you wish. When completed, sprinkle "snowdrifts" of sugar icing around for a final touch.

Note. This house may be kept for years if well wrapped in plastic and stored in a cool, dark, dry place.

Greenfield Village Apple Bread

Cream butter and sugar together and beat until fluffy. Beat eggs into butter-and-sugar mixture. Mix all dry ingredients together well. Add flour mixture and apples alternately to egg mixture, mixing well after each addition. Stir in lemon rind and walnuts. (Batter will be stiff.) Bake in greased and floured 9×5×3-inch loaf pan at 350° for approximately 1 hour. Remove from oven. After 5 minutes remove from pan and cool on a rack.

  Note. Do not slice until cold. This bread is delightful when toasted.

¼ cup butter, softened
⅔ cup sugar
2 eggs, well beaten
2 cups flour
1 teaspoon baking powder
1 teaspoon baking soda
1 teaspoon salt
2 cups finely chopped
 apples (peeled and cored)
grated rind of 1 lemon
⅔ cup finely chopped
 walnuts

Greenfield Village Pumpkin Bread

Combine all dry ingredients (except sugar, nuts, and raisins) and mix well. Cream butter and sugar together. Add eggs and pumpkin and beat well. Add dry ingredients and milk alternately to creamed-butter mixture, beating well after each addition. Lightly flour both nuts and raisins and fold into batter. Pour batter into 9×5×3-inch loaf pan. Bake at 350° for 50–60 minutes. Leave bread in pan for about 10 minutes and then cool on a wire rack.

2 cups flour
2 teaspoons baking powder
½ teaspoon baking soda
1 teaspoon salt
1 teaspoon cinnamon
½ teaspoon ground cloves
½ teaspoon freshly grated
 nutmeg
¼ teaspoon ginger
½ cup butter, softened
1 cup brown sugar, tightly
 packed
2 eggs
1 cup cooked pumpkin
 (canned may be used)
½ cup milk
2 tablespoons flour
½ cup chopped walnuts
½ cup raisins

Greenfield Village
New York Cupcakes

Place butter and milk in small saucepan and heat slowly until butter melts; pour into large bowl. Stir lightly beaten eggs into milk-and-butter mixture. Mix dry ingredients together and blend into liquid mixture. Add wine and mix well. Half fill greased muffin tins and bake at 350° for approximately 25 minutes. Makes about twenty-four 2-inch cakes. Serve with Warm Cream Sauce (recipe on page 89).

½ cup butter
⅔ cup milk
3 eggs, lightly beaten
2½ cups flour
1½ cups sugar
½ nutmeg, grated (or 1 teaspoon grated)
½ teaspoon cinnamon
2 teaspoons baking powder
½ cup white wine

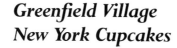

Greenfield Village
Apple Dumplings

Make pie crust according to your favorite recipe.

In small bowl, combine the 3 tablespoons butter, sugar, raisins, walnuts, and cinnamon; blend with fork.

Core apples. Pare apples and brush with lemon juice. Using spoon, fill hollows with raisin-walnut mixture.

Grease well a shallow baking pan.

On lightly floured surface, divide pastry evenly into six parts. Form each piece into a round ball. Flatten each piece; then roll out from center into an 8½-inch square. Trim edges, using pastry wheel. Save trimmings.

Place apple in center of each square; brush edges lightly with water. Bring each corner of square to top of apple; pinch edges of pastry together firmly, to cover apple completely.

Brush with yolk mixed with 1 tablespoon water. Bake at 400°, brushing once, halfway through baking time, with juices in pan, for 40 minutes, or until pastry is browned and apples are tender when tested with a toothpick. Makes six servings.

pastry for a 2-crust pie
3 tablespoons butter or margarine, softened
3 tablespoons sugar
1 tablespoon raisins
2 tablespoons chopped walnuts
¾ teaspoon cinnamon
6 large baking apples (Rome Beauty, Northern Spy)
2 tablespoons lemon juice
1 egg yolk

Greenfield Village Steamed Cherry Pudding

Mix all dry ingredients together. Blend well. Beat eggs well. Add milk, brandy, and melted butter. Beat well. Slowly add flour mixture to egg mixture, beating constantly. Carefully fold cherries into batter. Pour batter into greased and floured 2-quart mold or individual molds. Cover tightly with waxed paper. Place pudding on a rack in a large pot. Add enough boiling water to come halfway up the side of the mold. Regulate heat to keep water at a steady boil (add more boiling water as required). Cover pot, and steam large pudding approximately 2½ hours, individual puddings about 30 minutes. Serve with Warm Cream Sauce. Makes six servings.

¼ teaspoon ground cloves
¼ teaspoon grated nutmeg
¼ teaspoon ground ginger
2 teaspoons baking powder
1 teaspoon baking soda
½ teaspoon salt
2¼ cups flour
⅔ cup sugar
6 eggs
1½ cups milk
⅓ cup brandy
¼ pound (1 bar) butter, melted
1 pound dark pitted preserved cherries

Greenfield Village Eve's Pudding

Mix all dry ingredients together except sugar. Mix apples and suet together with raisins. Set aside. Beat egg yolks and sugar together. Add brandy. Combine egg-yolk mixture with dry ingredients, beating well. Fold fruit-and-suet mixture into batter. Beat egg whites until they form soft peaks. Gently fold egg whites into batter. Pour into greased 10-inch cake pan and bake at 350° approximately 1 hour. Serve with Warm Cream Sauce. Makes eight to ten servings.

1½ cups flour
1½ teaspoons baking powder
1 grated nutmeg
½ teaspoon salt
1 cup peeled chopped apples
1 cup finely chopped suet
1 cup raisins, dredged in flour
5 eggs, separated
1 cup sugar
⅓ cup brandy

Warm Cream Sauce

Melt butter and stir in sugar when butter has melted. Allow to become thick, stirring constantly over low heat. Add cream and whip gently with wire whisk. Add orange juice and whip. Grate nutmeg over sauce and serve.

¼ pound (1 bar) butter
⅔ cup superfine sugar
2 cups heavy cream
juice of 1 orange, strained
½ nutmeg, grated

Greenfield Village
Old-fashioned Popcorn Balls

Mix together corn syrup, sugar, water, and vinegar in a saucepan. Bring to a boil over medium heat, stirring constantly. Continue cooking, stirring occasionally, until temperature reaches 260° (hard-ball stage: a small quantity of the syrup dropped into ice water will form a ball that holds its shape but is still pliable).

Remove from heat and quickly stir in butter. Sprinkle popped corn with cinnamon. Slowly pour syrup over popped corn in a large bowl or pan, mixing well with a wooden spoon. Then, when mixture is still hot but can be handled safely, grease your hands well and shape it into balls about 2½ inches in diameter, using as little pressure as possible. Makes about thirty balls.

1 cup dark corn syrup
1 cup light brown sugar
¼ cup water
1 teaspoon white vinegar
2 tablespoons butter
4 quarts unsalted popped corn
cinnamon

Greenfield Village
Springerle Cookies

Beat eggs until light, gradually adding sugar, and continue beating for 15 to 20 minutes or until batter is thick and lemon-colored, like a soft meringue. Add anise seed. Combine flour and soda and blend with egg mixture. Cover bowl and let stand 15 minutes. This will make dough easier to work with. Divide into thirds. On lightly floured surface, roll dough to an 8-inch square, ¼ inch thick. Let rest 1 minute. Flour molds and press designs onto dough, cut, and place on a lightly floured surface. Cover with a towel overnight.

Grease a cookie sheet well. Dust with flour, and brush off excess. Align cookies, ½ inch apart, on sheet (they do not spread during baking). Bake about 15–20 minutes at 300°. Makes approximately twelve dozen cookies.

Note. Do not let cookies brown while baking. Store cookies in a tight container. Place a cut apple in the jar if cookies become too hard. Cinnamon (2 teaspoons) and ground cloves (1 teaspoon) can be used instead of the anise. The baking soda can be eliminated for a flatter cookie. This recipe can easily be halved.

8 eggs
4 cups sugar
8 tablespoons anise seed
8 cups flour
2 teaspoons baking soda

Cookies to Hang on the Tree and to Eat

Cream butter and sugar until fluffy and pale in color. Beat in eggs, liquor or vanilla, and mace. Gradually beat in 1 cup of the flour, and then work in the remainder until dough is smooth. Form into a ball and wrap in foil or plastic wrap, and place in refrigerator for 3 hours or overnight.

When dough is thoroughly chilled, press it out into a flat circle on a lightly floured surface. Then roll out 1/16 inch thick. Cut into desired shapes with cookie cutters. Place cookies on ungreased baking sheets and brush with egg-white mixture. Top with sugar sprinkles. Pierce each cookie near the top with a wooden skewer or toothpick so that a string for hanging can be inserted after baking (remember that holes tend to shrink during baking). Bake in a 375° oven until pale gold. Cool on racks. Yields about four dozen cookies.

Note. Cookies can also be decorated with colored sugar icing, if desired.

1 cup butter, softened
1 cup sugar
3 eggs, beaten
2 tablespoons brandy or whiskey, or 1 tablespoon vanilla
1 teaspoon ground mace
4 cups sifted flour
colored sugar sprinkles
2 egg whites, beaten with 2 tablespoons water

Nonedible Cookies to Hang on the Tree

Mix flour and salt. Slowly add water. Knead dough for 10 minutes, or until smooth. Roll out to less than 1/8-inch thickness on a floured surface. Cut into fancy shapes with cookie cutters. Place on lightly oiled baking sheet. Pierce top part of each cookie for hanging. Bake in a preheated 275° oven for 1¼ hours, or until totally hard and dry and pale gold in color. Cool on racks. Decorate with acrylic paints and glaze with clear varnish or polyurethane. Stored in a cool, dry place, these will keep from Christmas to Christmas. Yields about four dozen cookies. Remember, do not eat these cookies!

1 cup salt
4 cups flour
1½ cups water

Sugar-ring and paper-cutout cookies to hang on the tree.
Photograph by Bob Hanson

Donn Young Photography

TRADITIONS

The Gallier House

The Christmas season in the French Quarter of New Orleans was celebrated in the mid-nineteenth century among a profusion of delights, including camellia flowers, magnolia leaves, gilded pecans, and silk cornucopias filled with sugared almonds. Tables groaned under their load of rich Creole dishes and delicacies imported from the mother country, France. The family treasures of silver, fine china, and crystal were an integral part of the splendid holiday display, and they were set off by the elaborate decorations, such as the beaded silver poinsettias, that had been expertly crafted by the ladies of the household.

Christmas Eve and Christmas Day were marked by religious observances. On Christmas Eve no one failed to attend the *messe de minuit* (midnight mass). Afterward, young and old alike looked forward to the *réveillon*, the midnight supper that brought the family together for lively talk over a delicious repast. The very young retired to await Papa Noël, who would fill their stockings with small gifts.

During the holidays, the staff of the beautifully restored Gallier House faithfully recreates the opulent Creole Christmas of the 1860s. Among the unusual and striking decorations is the tree—a wax myrtle—festooned with gay colored ribbons and illuminated with small wax candles. This kind of tree, documented in an 1858 New Orleans newspaper, was very likely part of the Christmas celebration of James Gallier, Jr., an esteemed New Orleans architect, and his Spanish Creole wife.

Left: *The Gallier House's 1860s Christmas tree. Wax myrtle trees, placed on tabletops, were decorated with a multitude of lighted wax candles, cornucopias containing sugared almonds, gilded pecans, and many small ribbon bows.*
Courtesy Gallier House

Below: *The Royal Street facade of the Gallier House, a French Quarter townhouse built (1857–60) by noted New Orleans architect James Gallier, Jr.*
Courtesy Gallier House

Opposite: *A festive Gallier House front parlor. The Rococo Revival center table, set with an elegant coin-silver tea service, is ready for holiday callers.*
Donn Young Photography

Swags of evergreens decorate the Gallier House dining room—where the family gathered for the Christmas Eve post-midnight repast, the réveillon.
Donn Young Photography

On the mantel in the back parlor of the Gallier House, intricate glass-beaded poinsettias fill rare old Parisian vases, amid pine boughs and family treasures.
Donn Young Photography

REGIONAL CHRISTMAS TRADITIONS

By Victorian times, Santa Claus and the Christmas tree were attached firmly to the American holiday celebration. Religious groups that had once politely ignored Christmas began to take a second look, and regions that had turned their back on the day in early America were participating in Christmas merriment. At the same time, some of the distinctive characteristics of the festivities of New York, of the Pennsylvania Dutch country and neighboring areas of the mid-Atlantic region, of New Orleans and the rest of the South, and of the wide-open West were growing more sharply differentiated.

In the South

In Louisiana, as in many other corners of the country that made much of New Year's Day as an occasion for hospitality, the Nativity was not overlooked. There was no Santa Claus, no mistletoe, and no big Christmas dinner, because Christmas was considered mainly a religious festival. But—as in New Orleans's Gallier House every Christmas—homes were decorated with boxwood garlands, strands of woven holly, magnolia wreaths, camellias and gilded pecans, and intricately beaded flowers. Cooks kept a sort of liquid potpourri they called "odor punch" simmering on the stove throughout the holiday season; its wonderful scent of cinnamon, nutmeg, and other spices would fill an entire mansion. And on Christmas Eve there was the great midnight mass and the midnight supper—the *réveillon*—that followed.

All Louisianians, even those who never set foot in a church during the rest of the year, made a point of attending the *messe de minuit*. Glowing red candles, heaps of greenery, fragrant incense, the priests' and acolytes' glittering gold-and-white vestments, the cathedral's throaty chimes, and the thundering of the organ made this a very moving as well as an important social occasion. The *réveillon*, the Christmas Eve supper that followed, would include sweet rolls (perhaps filled with apples and almonds and spices), crisp loaves of bread, and the famous local specialty *daube glacé*, beef "taken on a trip to heaven" by the addition of such flavorings as bay leaf, cloves, garlic, onions, parsley, pepper, salt pork, sherry, thyme, and turnips. Other favorite dishes were bouillabaisse, pastry filled with pigeons, snipe on toast, and eggs in at least one form—in a soufflé, whipped into an omelet served with jelly, deviled with mushrooms, or baked with shrimp. Several wines were served, and also eggnog, usually hot.

For dessert, there were many choices: spiced peaches; dates soaked in port; honey cake; a layer cake filled with jelly, perhaps doused with wine or rum and mounded high with whipped cream; a rich *bûche de Noël*, a sponge cake filled with mocha buttercream, rolled like a jelly roll, and iced with chocolate. All these were very sweet and rich and were therefore perfect accompaniments for the strong, inky-black local coffee.

Late in the nineteenth century, the *réveillon* often continued until the dawn of Christmas Day. The children, who had been tucked into their beds long before the midnight service, rose early. After breakfast, on a sign from Maman, the servants threw open the doors to the parlor, where the children saw for the first time the family's small, glittering tree (the evergreen wax myrtle until late in the century, usually set on a tabletop), the *crèche* underneath, and their stockings filled with small trinkets and candies and cakes. Papa Noël, rotund as his Anglo-Saxon counterpart, traditionally put in an appearance and questioned the youngsters about their friends and relatives in ways that would set the whole family roaring with laughter. After his departure, it was usual for New Orleans youngsters to visit the city's cathedral and perhaps two or three smaller churches to see their *crèches*, each with its *p'tit Jésus*.

Christmas Goes West

The restless pioneers who left their well-tilled fields and comfortable homesteads behind to follow their dreams of freedom and prosperity into the wilderness were able to take with them few of their household goods. A single feather mattress, a well-polished cherrywood chest, a pewter candlestick might be the only material possessions that could be accommodated in the wagon or flatboat or steamer that took them west. But their customs and traditions traveled with them

Text continued on page 110

Above: *Gilded paper cornucopias, richly trimmed with satin braid and velvet, contain sugared almonds for visitors to the Gallier House.*
Courtesy Gallier House

Opposite: *A lavish holiday dessert table set in the restored dining room of the Hermann-Grima House in New Orleans.*
Courtesy Hermann-Grima House

As soon as the last note of the solemn midnight mass dies away, Creole families depart for home and a buoyant family gathering at the réveillon. This post-midnight repast is limited in scope but rich in its ingredients: eggs in one or two styles, daube glacé, galantines, gateaux, custards, several different wines, café noir, and perhaps a grand cream-puff pyramid, the dessert called "Croque-en-bouche."

The **Christmas Eve Réveillon** *menu incorporates information provided by the staffs of Gallier House, the Hermann-Grima House, and the Historic New Orleans Collection. Recipes, unless otherwise noted, are from the second edition (1901) of* The Picayune Creole Cook Book *(facsimile edition, Dover Books, 1971).*

A Christmas Eve Réveillon

Creole Eggnog

Eggs Scrambled with Preserves
(Oeufs Brouillés aux Confitures)

Creole Omelet
(Omelette à la Créole)

Baked Fish with Herb Stuffing
(Poisson au Four avec des Herbes)

Cold Beef à la Créole
(Daube Glacé)

———❊———

Jelly Cakes   Honey Cake
(Gâteaux aux Confitures)   *(Gâteau de Miel)*

Croque-en-bouche   Yule Log *(Bûche de Noël)*

Café Brûlot

Creole Eggnog

In a large bowl beat the egg yolks with the sugar until fluffy and pale in color. Place milk in a heavy saucepan and bring to a simmer over low heat. Watch carefully so that it does not boil over. Stir once or twice. While milk is heating, beat egg whites in another bowl until they stand in soft peaks. When milk is boiling hot, pour it over the egg-and-sugar mixture, whisking constantly.

Whisk in the brandy and then the beaten egg whites. Serve at once, while still warm, grating a little nutmeg over each serving. Makes about two and a half quarts, or about thirty to thirty-five servings.

10 eggs, separated
2 cups sugar
1 quart milk
1 cup French Cognac
freshly grated nutmeg

Eggs Scrambled with Preserves
(Oeufs Brouillés aux Confitures)

Break the eggs into a bowl. Add the marmalade. Have the frying pan very hot. Put into it the butter and immediately add the eggs, and keep stirring around and around and across for about three or four minutes, guided by the consistency of the egg (which must be like a thick mush as you take it from the fire). Keep stirring a few seconds longer after you have taken the pan off the fire, and put the eggs into a hot dish. The beauty of the scrambled egg is that the whites and yolks are delicately blended. The practice of beating the yolks and whites thoroughly together, as for an omelet, before scrambling the eggs is contrary to the principles of Creole cookery.

6 eggs
1 tablespoon butter
2 tablespoons fruit
  marmalade

Creole Omelet

(Omelette à la Créole)

Place 1 tablespoon of the butter in a small, heavy saucepan over moderate heat. When butter has melted, add the onions, garlic, bread crumbs, and ham. Sauté until golden brown, stirring occasionally. Then add the tomatoes, salt, pepper, and cayenne, and let all stew over low flame for about 1 hour, stirring from time to time.

If you wish to have the omelet very nice, beat the yolks in a small bowl until they are light in color. Beat the whites in a larger bowl until they form soft peaks, then beat the yolks into the whites.

Melt the remaining tablespoon of butter in a well-seasoned 10-inch omelet pan. Add the eggs. Let them cook over high heat for 2 minutes, shaking the pan back and forth vigorously enough to prevent sticking and to slide some of the uncooked egg onto the bottom of the skillet. Continue cooking and shaking until the eggs are set. Top of omelet should remain creamy. Immediately pour the tomato preparation over half the omelet, and then fold the other half of the omelet over it. Cook a few moments more and then slide omelet onto a warmed serving plate. Yields four servings, or six if presented as a first course.

2 tablespoons butter
2 medium onions, finely chopped
½ clove garlic, finely chopped
1 tablespoon fresh bread crumbs
2 tablespoons minced ham
6 fine ripe tomatoes, peeled, seeded, and chopped (or well-drained canned tomatoes, seeded and chopped)
salt to taste
freshly ground pepper to taste
pinch cayenne pepper, or more, to taste
6 eggs, separated

Baked Fish with Herb Stuffing

(Poisson au Four avec des Herbes)

Wipe fillets dry with a damp cloth or paper toweling. Chop together the garlic, parsley, scallions, mushrooms, and thyme. Mix with remaining ingredients. Spread half of this mixture over the fillets, fold fillets in half, and place in a shallow casserole or baking pan. Pour over the remaining herb mixture and marinate in a cool place for several hours. Bake in a 400° oven for 15 minutes, or until fish flakes easily. Serve at once, garnished with fresh lemon slices and additional parsley, if desired. Makes six servings.

Note. The original recipe, dated 1828, is for trout and calls for a whole fish, with the herbed mixture sewed into its cavity.

—*Hermann-Grima House*

2 pounds fish fillets (perch, red snapper, or trout)
2 cloves garlic
½ cup parsley sprigs
1 bunch scallions
1 cup small mushrooms
1 teaspoon thyme
¾ cup olive oil
juice of 1 lemon
1 scant teaspoon salt
½ teaspoon freshly ground pepper

Cold Beef à la Créole

(Daube Glacé)

The Jell

Place all the ingredients in a large pot or sauce-pan and cover with 3 cups of cold water; bring to a simmer, cover pot, and cook for 2½ hours. At the end of the first hour, remove veal chops, separate the meat from the bones and gristle, and return these to the pot. Mince veal very fine and reserve. While the above is cooking, prepare the beef.

2 pigs' feet, split
2 pounds thick-cut
  shoulder veal chops
1 teaspoon salt
freshly ground pepper
pinch cayenne pepper, or
  more, to taste
1 bay leaf, crushed
1 sprig thyme, or
  ½ teaspoon dried
1 clove garlic, chopped
2 whole garlic cloves,
  crushed
1 medium onion, chopped
½ cup dry sherry

The Beef

Press the cayenne, 1 chopped garlic clove, 1 tablespoon of the parsley, 1 sprig of the thyme (or ½ teaspoon of the dry thyme) into the salt pork strips. Cut incisions in beef and fill with herbed strips. Make insertions across the width of the meat, so that when it is sliced the strips will show in an attractive pattern.

Melt the lard over moderate heat in a large, heavy pot or enameled cast-iron casserole. Place beef in the pot, raise heat, and brown it on all sides. Drain off the lard and add 4 quarts of water and all the remaining ingredients. Cover pot, lower heat, and simmer about 4 hours.

5 pounds round, or a rump
  roast, in one piece
¼ pound salt pork, cut into
  thin strips, poached for
  20 minutes in 4 cups
  water, and drained
¼ teaspoon cayenne pepper
3 cloves garlic, finely
  chopped
½ cup parsley sprigs
5 sprigs fresh thyme, or
  2 teaspoons dried
2 tablespoons lard or other
  shortening
5 large onions, sliced
5 carrots, cut in 1-inch
  sections
2 medium turnips, cut in
  ½-inch cubes
¾ cup sherry or Madeira
salt, pepper, and cayenne
  to taste

To glacé the beef

After the pigs' feet have cooked for the full 2½ hours, or until tender, strain the cooking liquid into a bowl. Remove the bones from the pigs' feet and chop the meat coarsely. Add it and the reserved veal to the broth in the bowl.

Transfer the cooked beef to a casserole or serving dish slightly larger and deeper than the chunk of meat. Pour the prepared minced veal and broth over beef. Set casserole in refrigerator overnight. The broth will form a firm but tender jelly. Slice to serve, jelly and all. Makes eight to ten servings.

Jelly Cakes
(Gâteaux aux Confitures)

Cream butter and ½ cup of the sugar until fluffy and pale. Beat in the egg yolk, sour cream, vanilla (or rosewater), and brandy. Beat the egg white with the salt until it forms soft peaks and add the remainder of the sugar. Then gradually fold this mixture, alternately with the flour, into the butter mixture. Dissolve the baking soda in the milk and carefully fold into cake batter.

Grease two cupcake pans with softened butter, and sprinkle with flour. Place two tablespoons of batter into each depression and bake in a 350° oven for 10 minutes, or until the little cakes are light brown and shrink from the sides. Immediately turn out onto cake rack and cool.

Place a scant cup or so of preferred jelly in a small, heavy saucepan and stir until smooth. Sandwich each pair of cakes, bottoms facing, with a teaspoonful or so of jelly, and place them on the cake rack. When all have been sandwiched together, sift confectioners' sugar over the cakes, turning so that all sides are lightly coated. Makes about eighteen cakes.

⅓ cup butter, softened
⅔ cup sugar
1 egg, separated
⅓ cup sour cream
½ teaspoon vanilla (or 1 teaspoon rosewater)
1 teaspoon brandy
pinch salt
1⅓ cups sifted cake flour
⅛ (scant) teaspoon baking soda
2 tablespoons milk
currant, grape, or raspberry jelly
confectioners' sugar

Honey Cake
(Gâteau de Miel)

This is a very popular Creole cake. Mix honey and ¾ cup of the sugar in a bowl. Add the butter and the egg yolks. Beat hard until these ingredients are blended. Mix the baking powder, baking soda, and sifted flour together and sift again. Beat the egg whites in another bowl, and when they have formed soft peaks, beat in the remaining sugar. Alternately fold flour and egg whites into the honey mixture. Add the caraway seeds. Pour into a greased and floured 9×5×3-inch loaf pan. Bake in a 350° oven for 45 minutes. Makes one loaf.

1 cup honey
1 cup sugar
1 teaspoon melted butter
2 eggs, separated
1 teaspoon baking powder
pinch baking soda
2 cups sifted flour
1 teaspoon caraway seeds, if desired

Croque-en-Bouche

The French phrase meaning "to crunch in the mouth" aptly describes a dessert consisting of a cone-shaped arrangement of caramel-coated cream puffs.

Puffs

In a large, heavy saucepan, over moderate heat, melt the butter in the water. When liquid comes to a rolling boil, add all the flour and the salt. Stir vigorously until the mixture forms a solid mass and comes away from the sides of the pan. Remove from heat and allow to cool for 5 minutes. Using a wooden spoon, beat in the 8 eggs, one at a time, making sure batter is completely smooth after adding each egg.

When dough is satiny smooth, drop it by teaspoonfuls onto a greased cookie sheet, spacing them at least 1 inch apart. You will need two large cookie sheets; if you have only one, bake the puffs in relays. Smooth the mounds of dough into rounds with dampened fingers, brush each mound lightly with the egg-and-water mixture, and bake in a 400° oven for 20 minutes. Remove from oven and pierce each puff with the tip of a sharp knife to allow excess steam to escape (otherwise puffs will be soggy and might collapse) and return to oven for an extra 2 or 3 minutes. Place on racks to cool. When cool, fill each puff with Pastry Cream (see below), or sweetened whipped cream. (Puffs may remain unfilled for 24 hours, but once they are filled the Croque-en-bouche should be assembled immediately.) Makes from sixty to seventy small puffs.

1 cup (2 sticks or ½ pound) butter
2 cups water
2 cups flour
1 teaspoon salt
8 eggs
1 egg beaten with 2 tablespoons water

Pastry Cream

Beat sugar and egg yolks together until fluffy and pale in color. Beat in salt and flour until smooth and creamy. Gradually add the scalding milk. Place in a heavy saucepan and cook over low heat, whisking constantly. Mixture will soon thicken; continue to whisk until smooth. When very thick, remove from heat, pour into a bowl, and beat in the vanilla. Press plastic wrap onto surface of cream (to prevent a crust from forming) and chill thoroughly. (This may be prepared

¾ cup sugar
6 egg yolks
pinch salt
½ cup flour
2½ cups milk, scalded
2 teaspoons vanilla

24 hours in advance.) Yields about three and a half cups.

You are now ready to assemble the Croque-en-bouche. Fill each puff with pastry cream.

Caramel

Place sugar, cream of tartar, and water in a small, heavy saucepan. Stir over very low heat until sugar is dissolved. (Do not stir after this point has been reached.) Raise heat and allow sugar syrup to cook until it is a ruddy gold in color (345° on candy thermometer). Remove pan from stove at once, and place it in a larger pan containing boiling water, in order to keep caramel soft and manageable.

Lift each puff with tongs and dip the unpierced side into the syrup. Place syrup side down on a large round serving platter on which a thin layer of the syrup has been spread. When the first layer of puffs is complete, make a second layer, smaller in circumference. Keep on building up in this manner until a tall, tapered cone of puffs is formed. Makes twelve to fifteen servings.

Note. Take great care when working with caramel: it can cause serious burns. Also, make sure that the puffs are dipped on the unpierced side. Dipping them where they were pierced and filled will prove messy and will inhibit the hardening of the caramel.

3 cups sugar
pinch cream of tartar
½ cup water

Yule Log *(Bûche de Noël)*

Beat the egg yolks until lemon-colored. Beating constantly, slowly add ¾ cup of the sugar. Continue to beat for several more minutes, then slowly beat in the water, a tablespoonful at a time, and finally beat in the vanilla.

Place the egg whites and salt in another bowl. Beat for a few seconds, then add the cream of tartar. Continue beating until the whites form soft peaks. Slowly beat in the remaining ¼ cup sugar.

Resift the flour with the baking powder, and gradually add to the egg-yolk mixture, alternately folding in the beaten egg whites.

Butter an 11×17-inch jelly-roll pan and line with buttered and floured waxed paper. Pour cake batter into pan, smoothing it out evenly, and bake in a 350° oven for 15 minutes, or until cake is golden brown. Remove from oven, let sit for a minute, and then carefully turn cake upside down onto a dish towel that has been dusted with confectioners' sugar. Immediately peel off the waxed paper, taking care not to tear the cake. Trim off the crisp edges with a sharp knife, since they may cause the cake to crack when it is rolled. Sprinkle cake with a light sifting of confectioners' sugar, cover with a fresh sheet of waxed paper, and, starting with the short end, roll it up in the towel. While cake is cooling, prepare the butter cream.

4 eggs, separated
1 cup superfine sugar
5 tablespoons warm water
1½ teaspoons vanilla
pinch salt
pinch cream of tartar
1 cup sifted cake flour
½ teaspoon baking powder
3 tablespoons butter,
    softened
confectioners' sugar

Butter Cream

Beat the butter until fluffy, then gradually beat in the confectioners' sugar. Then beat in the egg yolks, one at a time; the cooled coffee solution, one tablespoon at a time; and the vanilla.

Carefully unroll the cooled cake, remove waxed paper, and spread it with about ½ inch of the butter cream. Roll it up again and place it on a serving dish. Add 3 tablespoons of the powdered cocoa to the remaining butter cream and beat it in thoroughly. Ice the surface of the roll, except for the ends, with this. With a fork, score the icing neatly from end to end so that it resembles the bark of a log. Sprinkle icing with the remaining tablespoon of cocoa and the pistachio nuts. Makes eight to ten servings.

—*Hermann-Grima House*

1 cup sweet butter, softened
2 cups confectioners' sugar,
    sifted
3 egg yolks
3 tablespoons instant coffee,
    dissolved in 2
    tablespoons hot water
    and cooled
1 teaspoon vanilla
4 tablespoons unsweetened
    cocoa
2 tablespoons coarsely
    chopped pistachio nuts

Donn Young Photography

Café Brûlot

In a brûlot bowl or the deep pan of a chafing dish, mash the cinnamon, cloves, peels, and sugar lumps with the back of a ladle or with a wooden spoon. Light the heating element and add the brandy and liqueur to the spices and peels. Heat for a minute or so, stirring constantly. Step back, and ignite the warmed spirits. Keep mixing, lifting the peels over the bowl with the ladle so that the burning spirits run down their length. When the sugar has dissolved, add the hot coffee. Continue to mix until the flames die out. Serve at once in special brûlot cups, mugs, or demitasses. Yields ten to twelve servings.

2 sticks cinnamon
12 whole cloves
peel of 2 oranges, each cut in a single continuous spiral
peel of 2 lemons, each cut in a single continuous spiral
24 sugar cubes ("Dots"), or 12 pieces lump sugar
1 cup brandy
¼ cup triple-sec or Curaçao
4 cups strong, hot, freshly brewed coffee (New Orleans type, with chicory, French roast, or espresso preferred)

Courtesy Conner Prairie Pioneer Settlement

Conner Prairie Settlement

Holiday visitors to Indiana's Conner Prairie Settlement, an authentically restored pioneer village in Noblesville, are treated to a glimpse of life in the village during Christmas 1836.

Since the scant population of the harsh Indiana frontier did not include any Hollanders, German Lutherans, or Anglicans, an old-fashioned Christmas with treats for St. Nick, gaily wrapped gifts, and decorated fir trees was not to be found on the Indiana prairie in 1836. Instead, the town's Methodists, Baptists, and Quakers would be continuing their preparation for the barren winter days ahead. At Whitaker's store there would be grumbling about the Cincinnati jobbers who suggested that the store carry Christmas items: "Folks around here have credits enough to pay off without buying fancy Christmas gifts."

The village potter, Asa Baker, being a good Quaker, would decline to join in any celebrations, but would forbear to criticize those who did. Dr. Campbell, whose wife was a Virginian, indulged her desire for Christmas decorations of red cedar boughs, and they would have a Christmas "at home," with eggnog and carol singing around the piano. From Indianapolis the prosperous William Conner, a member of the state legislature, would bring home fancy Christmas sweets and stories of holiday parties. For his homecoming on Christmas Eve, there would be a gala feast emphasizing the day's tradition of hospitality rather than its religious aspect.

Christmas was not declared an official holiday by the state of Indiana until 1875.

in their hearts, taking up no space in boat or wagon. Celebrating familiar holidays was one of the few luxuries they allowed themselves, a bulwark against the bitter homesickness that assailed them.

For many a pioneer, it was Christmas that was most eagerly anticipated, and the tales of Yuletide trials and hardships are all the more poignant for the fact. In the literature of the settling of the American West there are not a few stories of separated families, of sorrows and disappointments. But many difficult Christmases ended happily. On one Christmas Eve in

The barn and smokehouse in the village carpenter's yard; since this Conner Prairie family does not observe Christmas, there is no evidence of the holiday.
Courtesy Conner Prairie Pioneer Settlement

the West, a train bearing a widow and her two children to their grandmother's house for the promised celebration was caught in a fierce blizzard. The tracks finally became impassable, and as the trainman tramped on ahead to get a snowplow, it became clear to the children that there would be no Christmas at Grandma's for them. But the other passengers conspired to create a substitute. A cattleman lent the youngsters his brand-new socks to hang up. A salesman, traveling with a trunk full of trinkets made by the notions manufacturer he represented, supplied the glittering wherewithal to fill them. Two of the passengers waded through the prairie snow for a Christmas tree—and came back with a large branch of sagebrush, which the mother decorated with train lanterns and rosettes of tissue paper. When the trainman returned bringing a whole cooked turkey, the festivities were complete. The Reverend Cyrus Townsend Brady, who told the tale in his memoirs (published in 1901), observed that the children had probably never before had such a Christmas. "And to see the thin face of that mother flush with unusual color when we handed her one of those monstrous red plush albums . . . between the leaves of which the cattleman had generously slipped a hundred-dollar bill, was worth being blockaded for a dozen Christmases."

The settlers added variations of their own to the traditions of hospitality of their ancestors. Westward-bound Victorians took with them Santa Claus, their Christmas trees, and their greenery. An English botanist traveling in California during the Christmas of 1861 noted that evergreens decked churches and homes but remarked that they were not the cone-bearing trees he was accustomed to seeing in Sheffield, but redwood, which to him looked "exotic."

To Minnesota, Swedish settlers brought their Christmas cakes and their custom of setting out small sheaves of unthreshed wheat for the birds. Southerners exploded firecrackers wherever they were. In Boone County, Iowa, groups of men observed the custom of the shooters in the South. They got together on Christmas Eve and called on their neighbors; at each house, they fired their muskets all at once—making a noise that would reverberate across the hills—and then were invited in for coffee and pie.

And in St. Louis and some nearby sections of Missouri settled by the French, church bells pealed at midnight and called the inhabitants to midnight mass; even if the church was made of logs the altar was decorated with greens and illuminated with candles. An ample *réveillon*, not unlike those consumed in New Orleans, followed the mass.

The Conner Prairie Pioneer Settlement in Noblesville, Indiana, each year recreates frontier life

The soft glow of candlelight from punched-tin lanterns brightens a dark winter's night.
Courtesy Conner Prairie Pioneer Settlement

111

as it was carried on during the Christmas season of 1836. In the handful of households in the region that did celebrate Christmas during their first years in the wilderness, preparations began weeks beforehand, as in the East, but there were no silver candlesticks to polish, no crystal chandeliers to clean. The mistress of a two-room log cabin had only to shake out the rag rug that covered the dirt floor, whitewash the walls with lime, scrub the tables and chairs, and perhaps put up some evergreen boughs.

Pioneer couples did their best to make things festive for their offspring. In the absence of a store at which to buy toys, or of money with which to pay for them, a child might have to be content with pictures of his heart's desires snipped out of a mail-order catalogue. A fat brown doughnut, a pair of mittens, an apple, a piece of candy and a slate pencil, a bobsled made from a crate, a wooden six-shooter carved out of a bit of wood, a doll with a head carved from a raw potato, its hair made of strands from a horse's tail and its body of stuffed fabric—these are some of the presents remembered and recorded by pioneer children. The pink calico apron, the striped candy cane, the apple, and the china-headed doll received by one pioneer girl in 1861 were remembered for the rest of her life; the doll was the only one she ever received. Sometimes, there were no presents at all, and parents simply told their children that Santa Claus had had a bad year or that he had not yet found his way to their new home.

Many pioneer children also did without Christmas trees. The Victorians' Christmas tree fever notwithstanding, only about one out of every five American families had their own tree as of 1900. In the West and in some small towns in the South, trees in the home were unusual. If a child saw a tree at all, it was a Sunday school tree or a community tree like the one now set up annually at Columbia Village, California, a state-parks department restoration of a once-booming California gold-rush town.

Still, there were many pioneer families who went to considerable trouble in order to set up trees in their hard-won new dwellings. A North Dakota mother who could find no evergreens nearby chopped down a bare-limbed deciduous tree, stood it up next to the front door, and doused it with water, which froze into delicate glistening icicles. A German

At the smokehouse, a supply of wood is being laid in for the smoking of meat. Indiana winters are unpredictable and often bitterly cold, and villagers had to be totally prepared for months during which there were no readily available outside food sources.
Courtesy Conner Prairie Pioneer Settlement

Text continued on page 123

Top: *Much in evidence at Christmastime are preserving jars for containing peach and apple butter, jams, and pickled foods (such as onions and beef tongue), and jugs for holding rhubarb or berry wine.*
Courtesy Conner Prairie Pioneer Settlement

Left: *Conner Prairie Christmas dinners were prepared in the kitchen fireplace; if it lacked a clock jack to run the rotisserie, the children of the house took turns slowly rotating the meat as it cooked over the fire.*
Courtesy Conner Prairie Pioneer Settlement

Above: *In the Conner Prairie Settlement's Campbell House, holiday preparations are more elaborate than in most Indiana homes of this period.*
Courtesy Conner Prairie Pioneer Settlement

Opposite: *Preparing Christmas dinner in one of the more affluent Conner Prairie households.*
Courtesy Conner Prairie Pioneer Settlement

By 1835, cooking on the prairie had become more "refined." A meal was no longer a one-pot affair, with or without corn bread. All food was cooked either over or in front of the fire. Once lit, a fire was never allowed to go out; at night it would be banked. If the fire was just right, a roast could be satisfactorily cooked on a spit in front of it, allowing sixteen minutes to the pound.
The **Frontier Christmas Bill of Fare** *was derived from information provided by the staff of the Conner Prairie Pioneer Settlement, which has done extensive research on prairie life in the 1830s. The recipes are from Conner Prairie, except for two which are from* Recipes from America's Restored Villages *by Jean Anderson (Doubleday & Company, Inc. © 1975).*

Frontier Christmas Bill of Fare

Rhubarb or Berry Wine

Hoosier Biscuits

Skillet Cranberries

Roast Goose with Indiana Sauce

Candied Orange Bowls

Sugar Cake   Apple Frazes

Holiday desserts included cakes, cookies, puddings, and fruits such as apples and store-bought oranges. Cheese, pumpkin,
and mincemeat pies, prepared either in the beehive oven or in a spider on the hearth, were also popular.
Courtesy Conner Prairie Pioneer Settlement

Hoosier Biscuits

Place the milk in a warm large mixing bowl, stir in salt and yeast, and mix until both are dissolved. Stir in 3 cups of the flour, 1 cup at a time, to make a stiff batter. Cover with a clean dry cloth and set in a warm spot, away from drafts, to rise for about 1½ hours, or until doubled in bulk. Stir the batter down; mix in the baking soda solution and then the eggs. Mix in the remaining 3½ cups flour, 1 cup at a time, to form a stiff dough (it will still be slightly sticky).

Turn dough out onto a well-floured board, sprinkle top lightly with flour, and flour your hands also. Knead the dough hard for about 5 minutes, just until it is springy and satiny smooth, adding a little extra flour as needed to keep the dough from sticking to the board and to your hands. Place in a buttered large mixing bowl, and turn dough in the bowl so that it is buttered all over. Cover with cloth and let rise 45 minutes in a warm spot, away from drafts, until not quite doubled in bulk.

Punch dough down, turn out onto a lightly floured board and roll out to a thickness of ½ inch. Cut into rounds with a floured 2½-inch biscuit cutter, then place biscuits ½ inch apart on ungreased baking sheets. Again cover with cloth and let rise about 1 hour in a warm spot—just until the biscuits have about doubled in height. Bake in a moderately hot oven (375°) until lightly browned on top, about 15 minutes. Serve piping hot with plenty of butter. Makes about two and a half dozen.

—*America's Restored Villages*

2 cups milk, scalded and cooled to lukewarm
1 teaspoon salt
2 tablespoons active dry yeast
6½ cups sifted all-purpose or unbleached flour (about)
1 teaspoon baking soda, dissolved in ¼ cup hot water
2 eggs, beaten until frothy

Skillet Cranberries

Spread cranberries in an ovenproof skillet. Sprinkle sugar over them. Cover and place in a 225° oven. After 1 hour, remove the lid and pour brandy over the cranberries. Makes about three cups.

1 pound cranberries
2 cups sugar
¼ cup brandy

Roast Goose with Indiana Sauce

Rinse cavity of the goose. Stuff with sage and onions that have been mixed with salt and pepper. (Rinse the sage and onions in a little water before they are chopped or mix a few bread crumbs with them when chopped to render them less strong.) Rub the skin of the goose with butter. Place on rack in open pan and roast at 325° until tender, about 30 minutes per pound. Turn goose as it roasts, to brown evenly. Goose is cooked if juices from the thigh run clear when it is pierced with a fork. Makes six servings.

1 8–10-pound goose
6–8 sage leaves
2 onions, chopped
2 teaspoons salt
1 teaspoon pepper
1 tablespoon butter, softened

Indiana Sauce

Mix ingredients and put in jar. Let sauce stand for a week, then pass it through a sieve and bottle it up securely. This sauce is excellent for game or broiled cutlets.

—*Mrs. Collins' Table Receipts, Adapted to Western Housewifery,* 1851

4 tablespoons fresh-scraped horseradish
2 tablespoons dry mustard
2 tablespoons salt
2 teaspoons celery seed
2 onions, minced
½ teaspoon cayenne pepper
2 cups vinegar

Candied Orange Bowls

Cut oranges through the middle. Squeeze out the juice and peel away the pulp. Place rinds in cooking pot, cover with water, and bring to a boil. Cover and simmer for an hour. Put sugar and 1 cup water in another pot and boil for 5 minutes. Add rinds and cook slowly for 2 hours. Uncover and cook another hour. Remove from pot and roll in sugar. Cool on racks. Makes eight "bowls."

4 large oranges (well scrubbed)
2½ cups sugar

Sugar Cake

Mix sugar into hot mashed potatoes. Add salt, yeast, butter, lard, and eggs, stirring well after each addition. Sift flour and add to mixture, stirring until smooth. Cover and let rise 5 hours. Spoon into 4 greased 9-inch pie tins or a Turk's head mold (a round, deep pan with hole in center). Let rise 1 hour, or until doubled. Punch

1 cup sugar
1 cup hot dry mashed potatoes
¾ teaspoon salt
2 tablespoons dry active yeast, dissolved in ¼ cup warm water

holes about an inch apart in dough and insert chips of cold butter. Push butter down into dough, adding some brown sugar and cinnamon. Sprinkle more sugar on top. Bake in a 350° oven until done. Makes about fifteen servings.

½ cup melted butter
¼ cup melted lard
3 eggs, beaten
4 cups flour
¼ pound cold butter, cut into small pieces
brown sugar
cinnamon

Apple Frazes

Core the apples, peel, and slice about ⅜ inch thick. Brown lightly on both sides in the butter in a large, heavy skillet over moderately high heat, allowing 1 to 2 minutes per side; drain apple slices on paper toweling.

3 large, not too tart, cooking apples (McIntosh, Jonathan, and Winesap are good varieties to use)
3 tablespoons butter
flour (for dredging apple slices)

Batter

To prepare the batter: Beat the eggs, egg yolks, and sugar in an electric mixer at high speed until very thick and light—about 3 minutes of hard beating should do it. Stir together the flour and nutmeg; combine the cream, sherry, and melted butter. Then add the flour mixture to the beaten eggs alternately with the combined liquids, beginning and ending with flour.

Dredge the apples lightly on both sides with flour (simply dip them in a small bowl of flour, shaking off any excess flour), then dip in the batter to coat evenly. Fry on a lightly greased, large griddle over moderate to moderately high heat, just until lightly browned on each side. This will take about 1 to 2 minutes on each side—the slices are ready to turn when small holes appear in the surface of the batter.

3 eggs
2 egg yolks
4 tablespoons sugar
1 cup sifted all-purpose flour
½ teaspoon ground nutmeg
3 tablespoons heavy cream at room temperature
3 tablespoons dry sherry
1 tablespoon melted butter

Topping

Serve the frazes griddle-hot and top each with a generous ladling of melted butter and with a heaping teaspoon of granulated sugar or thick dusting of sifted confectioners' sugar. Makes six servings.

melted butter
granulated sugar or sifted confectioners' sugar

—*America's Restored Villages*

The St. Charles Saloon in Columbia ready for a "Miner's Christmas Celebration."
Union Democrat Photograph

Columbia

We sent word up and down creek that we would celebrate Christmas at our camp and everybody bring some grub and a fiddle if he had one. Christmas morning they were all there demanding a showdown. We had a fat grizzly and a deer. . . . A sailor yelled, "Let me make the plum duff, maties," and he did.

Beans and bacon—and one man brought two pickles, which were carefully divided up into slices between eleven men.

Rover, our dog, took the place of a watcher that would have charged three ounces a night to guard the gold, so we figured he saved us about forty dollars a night and fed him accordingly.

—A California Forty-niner

In the year 1850, in the heart of the Mother Lode, Dr. Thaddeus Hildreth, his brother, and a few other prospectors found gold. Within weeks, Hildreth's diggings became a tent-and-shanty town of several thousand miners. By 1855 this new town, now called Columbia, held a rip-roaring Christmas ball. Today Columbia, a California State Park, celebrates in the spirit of the camaraderie of the miners, and everyone is invited to participate in a nineteenth-century miners' Christmas, complete with dinner at the City Hotel, Santa arriving by stagecoach, and a candlelight parade.

Above: *Dressing a forty-niner Christmas tree at Columbia.*
Photograph by Robert Westgate

Right: *Columbia's Candy Kitchen in full swing testifies that even crusty miners are not exempt from the sweet tooth.*
Photograph by Robert Westgate

Above: *Columbia's children play an active part in staging the "Miner's Christmas Celebration."*
Photograph by Robert Westgate

The lure of the gold in them thar hills gives way, at holiday time, to the urge to make a fine gingerbread house.
Photograph by Robert Westgate

settler in St. Clair County, Illinois, made up for the lack of evergreens in another way. He hung his ornaments—bright paper, nuts, red apples and berries, sweets, and ribbons—on the branches of a sassafras bush and then lighted it with candles.

For ornaments, chestnuts and other natural products served. One Swedish immigrant family too poor to buy ornaments hung their silverware on their tree. Farm boys stuffed the squirrels, chipmunks, and other small game that they had bagged during the year and attached them to the branches or placed them underneath the tree. If there were supplies enough to make cookies, huge ones cut in the shapes of farmyard animals were favored. A dexterous whittler could fashion wooden candle holders to be fastened to the branches with yarn.

The menu of the frontier Christmas dinner was determined by individual resources. One Christmas, two young cowpokes guarding sheep on the range ate nothing because a dog ran off with the head of a wild pig that they had put aside for their dinner. A pair of British gold miners in a Sierra Nevada camp, reminiscing about the feasting taking place at home, decided to pretend that their pot of coffee was eggnog; they sang some songs, smoked their pipes, and thought themselves happy. A family who usually ate only corn bread and potatoes—"and a few potatoes at that," in the words of the missionary who left us the record—considered a meal that contained a bit of ham more than bountiful. Another family, having just spent long months crossing the country on the Oregon Trail, was similarly hard put to it to find more than flour, potatoes, some dried fruit, a little brown sugar, and some bacon when the holidays rolled around.

In an area of plenty such as Iowa, in a good year, not only turkey, roast venison, and roast pork but also potatoes, nuts, maple sugar, and mince pie (made with berries gathered during the warmer months and then dried) graced the Christmas table. A surveying party living mainly off the land in Texas in 1872 laid out a festal board with many varieties of meat and fowl: antelope, bacon hauled from five hundred miles away, bear, brant goose, buffalo, curlew, deer, ducks, possum, prairie chicken, prairie dog, quail, rabbit, and turkey. The offer of rattlesnakes and polecats made by one of the party was declined.

Minnesota records describe a family Christmas dinner of stewed oysters, boiled vegetables, baked pork and beans, cranberry and mince pies, cheese and nuts. Another menu lists wild goose, venison, coon, five kinds of cake, three varieties of pie, and doughnuts fried in coon's grease. Yet another holiday dinner featured prairie chicken, venison, and bear meat furnished by a friendly Indian chief, who joined the recipients after dinner for races, dances, and a ball game.

As the West lost its wildness, pioneer Christmas celebrations came to approximate the festivities of the East. Wealthier families in some areas could afford a turkey, though they were often expensive: in mid-nineteenth century St. Paul they sold for the then astronomical sum of $1.50 to $2.00, since they had to be brought by sleigh from Iowa and Illinois.

The local newspapers advertised Christmas balls "gotten up with as much elegance and taste as can be displayed in any of the great cities." A given region's fine fashion, genteel and accomplished men, beautiful women and girls, cotillions, parties, ladies' fairs, and other worldly attractions were also lauded in holiday issues. One Christmas season in nineteenth-century St. Paul was described as "rich in social entertainments and interesting exercises." An amateur theatrical performance of *Uncle Tom's Cabin* was presented on Christmas Day of 1874 in the opera house in Winterset, Iowa. Elsewhere in Iowa, residents of Sioux City were offered a Christmas Day matinee performance by a Professor Nickle, billed as "the world-renowned illusionist." Admission was a dollar for a family of six.

Churches were "banked with evergreens" and "ablaze with the light of gas burners and tapers" for the holidays. Frequently there were parties in the Sunday schools. A handsome tree would be set up, glittering with lighted candles and laden with presents. The tree, the presents, the good things to eat, the special program of recitations, tableaux, and carol singing inspired more than one child to bemoan the fact that Christmas came but once a year.

Courtesy Library of Congress

Opposite (above): *Located in the heart of the Mother Lode, at the base of the western edge of the Sierra Nevada, Columbia yielded—at nineteenth-century prices—$87 million in gold.* Photograph by Robert Westgate

Opposite (below): *The Christmas tree at the St. Charles Saloon is decorated with typical Victorian ornaments.* Photograph by Robert Westgate

The nation's first Christmas was as triumphant as its Declaration of Independence. The English General Howe and his Hessian soldiers were celebrating the holiday in 1776 with the feasting to which they were accustomed—and General George Washington took advantage of the situation, stealing Indian-wise across the ice-clogged Delaware River to take his foes by surprise and defeat them.

In 1789, George Washington, now the nation's first president, spent Christmas not at Mount Vernon—where he had enjoyed many holidays in the manner of the Virginia country gentleman that he was—but in New York. "The visitors to Mrs. Washington this afternoon were not numerous," he noted in his diary entry for that day, "but respectable." Twenty dignitaries feasted on roast beef, veal, turkey, duck, chicken, and ham, followed by pudding, jellies, oranges, apples, almonds and other nuts, raisins, figs, wines, and punches—all served at a long, elegantly set table, with the only lady present, Mrs. Washington, presiding. Toasts all around completed the meal: "To all our friends," the General would habitually say, saluting his guests.

Washington never spent a Christmas in the White House, which was not finished during his terms of office. So the honor of spending the first Christmas in the presidential mansion went to John and Abigail Adams, who had moved in only a month before the holiday commenced, with "not a chamber . . . finished of a whole!" and the closest water some six blocks away, much to Mrs. Adams's consternation. Her efforts to dry out the new plaster by burning some twenty cords of wood were in vain, and her guests shivered—and departed early.

From the very beginning of its celebration in America, Christmas was considered a special time for children. And so it was in the White House. The Adams's party for small fry was more successful—at least until the cup of one child's tea set was broken, and the nose of another child's doll was attacked by way of retaliation. That year, and for many years thereafter, the children in the White House were the liveliest part of the celebration.

In 1805, the widower Thomas Jefferson invited his six grandchildren—and a hundred other youngsters—to the mansion and himself played the violin for the dancing. When Andrew Jackson came to the White House, in 1829, still mourning the death of his wife, Rachel, his family put up a stocking for him and stuffed it with small gifts, including a corncob pipe. His nieces and nephews coaxed from their mammy some stockings "as capacious as the Galilee fishermen's nets she often referred to"—and, in the morning, found them filled with cakes and candy, nuts and fruit, and at least one doll. The same year, President Jackson, an erstwhile orphan, gave a holiday party for other orphans, complete with candies, cakes, ices shaped like apples and pears to eat, and snowballs made of starch-powdered cotton to throw. In the same vein, Abraham Lincoln's son Tad rounded up a crowd of street waifs and brought them home for turkey dinners.

Until the time of Franklin Pierce, who hailed from New Hampshire, where Christmas had been virtually ignored until a few years earlier, there were no Christmas trees in the White House. Pierce changed all that in 1856, and brought the nation one step closer to adopting the "German tree" when he set one up for a party that he and his wife planned for the New York Avenue Presbyterian Church Sunday School.

By the time Benjamin Harrison brought his father, his son and daughter, and his grandchildren to live in the White House, in 1889, the celebration of Christmas in America had developed enough so that the Chief Executive could call the holiday "the most sacred religious festival of the year." He helped decorate the White House himself in 1892, when his granddaughter's scarlet fever kept him quarantined. Electric lights, which had been introduced about 1882, were decidedly new-fangled—the *New York Times* had attacked them at least once—but Grover Cleveland, who succeeded Harrison in 1885, put them on his tree, right along with the winged gold angels, silver and gold sleds, and all manner of toys and tinsel.

THE PRESIDENTS

Courtesy The White House

The Christmas tree was by this time so popular in America that there was concern about the inroads on the nation's forests. As a staunch conservationist, Theodore Roosevelt felt impelled to proscribe an official Christmas tree, and in 1905, for the first time in years, there was no tree in the White House. But Roosevelt's youngsters could not imagine the holiday without a tree. The President's sister, who was not under the prohibition, took pity on her nieces and nephews and gave a Christmas party for them—complete with tree. The following year, the children determined to set up their own tree despite the parental decree. But the secret evergreen in a bedroom closet came to light, and Roosevelt mandated a visit to the nation's first professional conservationist, Gifford Pinchot, thinking that Pinchot would open his children's eyes to the wrongheadedness of Christmas trees. However, Pinchot told the boys that scientifically cutting Christmas trees could actually benefit timberlands, and Roosevelt had to concede.

During the Coolidge administration, the first lady decorated the windows with laurel wreaths tied with scarlet ribbons, in the best Victorian style. A huge wreath with pine cones and red berries—illuminated at night with tiny electric lights—was hung on the front door. In addition, there was not one tree but several—with a Nativity scene on a platform in the East Room nearby. Nationwide, the tree was so integral a part of the holiday festivity that it seemed entirely appropriate to inaugurate a National Christmas Tree. The lighting ceremony was broadcast on the radio for the first time in 1925.

Franklin Delano Roosevelt officiated at one of the nation's most memorable White House Christmases. In 1941, for the first time in many years, statesmen rather than children surrounded Commander-in-Chief Roosevelt over the holidays. With Pearl Harbor still fresh in American minds, the shocked nation had joined Britain in the battle against Hitler, and Prime Minister Winston Churchill had come to Washington for a series of conferences. United in a great cause and a beloved tradition, the two leaders stood side by side for the lighting of the National Christmas Tree.

Above: *A place setting on George and Martha Washington's dinner table, with a silver-plated centerpiece, Angoulême biscuit-porcelain ornaments, and silk flowers imported from France.*
Courtesy the Mount Vernon Ladies' Association

Opposite: *A small storage room at Mount Vernon containing a portion of the Washingtons' china.*
Courtesy the Mount Vernon Ladies' Association

In the prevailing fashion, dinner at Mount Vernon was served in three courses and on two tablecloths (one for each of the first two courses); the fruit, nuts, and wines were served on the bare table. In the center was an elegant épergne, and handsome platters containing meat and fish were placed symmetrically about the table. Dinners were customarily concluded with toasts all around.
    The **George Washington Dines at Mount Vernon** *menu is a composite, comprising dishes that were served at Mount Vernon in winter. Menu and recipes are from* The American Heritage Cookbook *(American Heritage Publishing Co., Inc. © 1971).*

George Washington Dines at Mount Vernon

An Onion Soup Call'd The King's Soup*

Oysters on the Half Shell   Broiled Salt Roe Herring   Boiled Rockfish

Roast Beef* and Yorkshire Pudding*   Mutton Chops

Roast Suckling Pig   Roast Turkey with Chestnut Stuffing*

Boeuf Bouilli with Horseradish Sauce*   Cold Baked Virginia Ham

Lima Beans   Baked Acorn Squash   Baked Celery with Slivered Almonds*

Hominy Pudding*   Candied Sweet Potatoes*

Cantaloupe Pickle*   Spiced Peaches in Brandy*   Spiced Cranberries

Mincemeat Pie*   Apple Pie*   Cherry Pie   Chess Tarts

Blancmange   Plums in Wine Jelly   Snowballs   Indian Pudding*

Great Cake*   Ice Cream   Plum Pudding

Fruits   Nuts   Raisins

Port   Madeira

*Recipe follows.

An Onion Soup Call'd The King's Soup

This recipe is adapted from The Lady's Companion, *a cookbook published in 1753, which was owned by Martha Washington.*

Place onions, milk, mace, butter, and salt in a saucepan. Bring to a boil, then reduce heat and cook slowly for 30 to 40 minutes, or until onions are very tender. Pick out mace blades and discard. Beat egg yolk in a small bowl, then add a little of the hot soup, beating constantly. Pour egg mixture into soup and cook a minute or two to thicken slightly. Sprinkle each serving with finely chopped parsley, then add a few croutons. Serves four.

2 large Bermuda onions, thinly sliced
1 quart milk
½ teaspoon mace blades
½ cup (1 stick) butter
1½ teaspoons salt
1 egg yolk
chopped parsley
croutons

To Roast Standing Ribs of Beef

This recipe is taken from Mary Ronald's Century Cook Book *(1895).*

"To roast beef on a spit before the fire is unquestionably the best method of cooking it; but as few kitchens are equipped for roasting meats, baking them in the oven is generally practised, and has come to be called roasting. Beef should be well streaked with fat, and have a bright-red color. Place the meat to be baked on a rack which will raise it a little above the bottom of the pan. Dredge the whole, top and sides, with flour. Place in a corner of the pan a half teaspoonful of salt and a quarter teaspoonful of pepper. Do not let them touch the raw meat, as they draw out the juices. Put into the pan also two tablespoonfuls of drippings. Place it in a very hot oven for fifteen or twenty minutes, or until the meat is browned; then shut off the drafts and lower the temperature of the oven, and cook slowly until done; baste frequently; do not put water in the pan, as it makes steam, and prevents browning. A roast has a better appearance if the ribs are not too long."

By suggesting that you start the roast at a high temperature, and then lower it, the author follows the French, or searing, method of roasting. Preheat the oven to 450°, then lower it to 325°.

The beef should be brought to room temperature before roasting. To cook a rib roast rare, allow 16 to 18 minutes per pound; medium rare, 18 to 22 minutes per pound; well done, 23 to 28 minutes per pound. Do not baste. Salt and pepper the meat after it has finished roasting and stand it on a warm platter 10 to 15 minutes before carving. This helps the juices to settle and makes the meat easier to carve.

Thermometer method of roasting: Insert thermometer in the fleshiest part of the roast, making sure it does not touch the bone. Place roast in a preheated 325° oven and roast, without basting, until thermometer reaches 140° for rare; 160° for medium; 170° for well done.

To roast rolled ribs of beef: Place the roast, fat side up, on a rack in the roasting pan and roast as you would a standing rib. Allow an additional 5 to 10 minutes per pound since the bone in a standing rib roast transmits heat and, consequently, the meat roasts more quickly.

Yorkshire Pudding

Heat an 8 × 10-inch baking pan in the oven, then pour in ¼ cup beef drippings. Move the pan back and forth until the bottom is well covered. Beat the eggs until very light and fluffy, then beat in the milk and flour, a little at a time. Add a generous pinch of salt and 2 tablespoons beef drippings. Pour the egg mixture into the prepared baking pan and bake in a preheated 450° oven for 10 minutes. Reduce heat to 350°, and bake 10 to 15 minutes longer or until pudding is puffy and delicately browned. Serve immediately to four.

2 eggs
1 cup milk
1 cup flour (scant)
salt
beef drippings

Chestnut Stuffing

Make a gash in the flat side of each chestnut, place them in a saucepan with boiling water to cover, and simmer for about 5 minutes. While nuts are still hot, remove shells and inner brown skins. Cover chestnuts with more boiling water and cook slowly for 20 to 30 minutes or until tender. Drain and chop coarsely. Melt butter in a saucepan, add onions and celery, and sauté until limp. Add bread crumbs to vegetable-butter combination and mix thoroughly. Then add salt, thyme, marjoram, and savory, mixing them in well. Add the chestnuts. This is enough stuffing for a 12–15-pound turkey.

2 pounds chestnuts
1½ cups (3 sticks) butter
2 cups onion, chopped fine
2 cups thinly sliced celery
9 cups fine dry bread
    crumbs
2 teaspoons salt
1 teaspoon dried thyme
1 teaspoon dried
    marjoram
1 teaspoon dried savory

Boeuf Bouilli

This recipe for boiled beef is adapted from one prepared by Étienne Lemaire, Jefferson's steward in Washington.

Place the meat in a heavy kettle, then add all the ingredients *except the salt.* Cover with water, bring to a boil, and boil for 5 minutes. Skim off froth, then add salt. Cover, lower the heat, and simmer 2 to 2½ hours or until meat is very tender when pierced with a fork. Potatoes and cabbage are especially compatible with boiled beef and may be cooked separately or added to the meat for the last hour. When meat is tender, lift from the broth, place on warm platter, and surround with cooked vegetables. Serve with Horseradish Sauce or tomato sauce with horseradish added to taste. Serves six.

4 to 5 pounds lean beef
    (first cut brisket, bottom
    round, or plate beef)
1 large onion, stuck with 6
    cloves
3 carrots, cut in chunks
3 to 4 stalks celery with
    leaves
1 white turnip, quartered
1 parsnip, cut in chunks
    (optional)
parsley
4 to 5 peppercorns
1 tablespoon salt

Horseradish Sauce

Mix mustard with 1 tablespoon cold water, stir until smooth, then combine with horseradish, salt, and pepper. Allow to stand for 10 minutes. Fold thoroughly into the whipped cream. Excellent with hot or cold meats, especially beef or tongue. Makes one cup.

½ teaspoon dry mustard
6 tablespoons freshly
    ground horseradish
1 teaspoon salt
½ teaspoon white pepper
½ cup heavy cream,
    whipped

Baked Celery with Slivered Almonds

Wash celery and cut into slices about ½ inch thick (save a generous handful of the celery tops). Place the celery in a saucepan, cover halfway with boiling, salted water, and lay the celery leaves on top. Cook for 10 to 15 minutes after water has reached the boiling point or until tender. Discard leaves and drain celery thoroughly, saving ½ cup of the celery water. While celery cooks, melt *2 tablespoons of the butter* in a saucepan, stir in flour until smooth, add milk. Cook over a low heat, stirring constantly, until smooth and bubbly. Stir in ½ cup celery water and taste to see if more salt is needed. Place a layer of the cooked celery in a shallow baking dish, spoon half the sauce over it, and sprinkle with half the almonds. Add the remaining celery, then the sauce. Sprinkle the top with bread crumbs, dot with the remaining butter, and sprinkle remaining almonds over all. Bake in a preheated 350° oven for 30 minutes. Serves four.

1 large bunch Pascal celery
4 tablespoons butter
2 tablespoons flour
1 cup milk
½ cup celery water
½ cup blanched, slivered almonds
2 tablespoons dry bread crumbs

Hominy Pudding

Hominy was adopted from the Indians and became an important basic food for American pioneers. It is, simply, hulled corn—the pioneers removed the hulls by soaking the grains of corn in a weak wood lye. Washed and boiled until it was tender, hominy was often served in place of potatoes.

Stir grits into boiling water. Cover and cook over a low heat for 25 to 30 minutes. Set aside to cool. Then measure exactly 2 cups of the cooled grits into a bowl and beat until smooth. Beat yolks soundly and stir into grits. Add cream, salt, and pepper. Beat egg whites until they stand in peaks and fold into grit mixture, lightly but thoroughly. Spoon into a well-buttered 1-quart casserole and bake in a preheated 350° oven for 40 minutes or until surface is golden. Serve immediately to four.

1 cup hominy grits
5 cups boiling water
2 eggs, separated
½ cup light cream
1 teaspoon salt
¼ teaspoon white pepper

Candied Sweet Potatoes

Sweet potatoes (the dark orange variety are often called yams) have been grown in this country since at least the early seventeenth century and are associated with Southern cooking.

Cook the sweet potatoes in their jackets in boiling, salted water until nearly tender. Drain, peel, and cut in slices about ½ inch thick. Place in a greased, shallow baking dish and sprinkle with salt. Cook together brown sugar, water, and butter in a separate pan for several minutes. Then stir in lemon juice and pour over potatoes. Bake in a preheated 375° oven for 20 to 25 minutes, basting occasionally with the syrup. Serves four to six.

6 sweet potatoes
½ teaspoon salt
1 cup dark brown sugar
½ cup water
4 tablespoons butter
1 tablespoon lemon juice

Cantaloupe Pickle

Peel a large unripe cantaloupe, remove seeds and membrane, cut into small pieces. Cover with white vinegar, then pour off all the vinegar and measure it. To every pint of vinegar add 1¾ cups of brown sugar (firmly packed), 8 whole cloves, ½ teaspoon cinnamon, and ¼ teaspoon mace. Bring the mixture to a boil. Add melon and cook over a low heat until tender and almost transparent. With a slotted spoon, transfer cantaloupe to a bowl. Continue to boil pickling liquid for about 12 minutes. Pour over melon. Cool completely before using. Makes about one quart.

Spiced Peaches in Brandy

Stick one clove in each peach and place in saucepan with the juice. Add cinnamon and mace and simmer gently until heated through. With a skimmer, remove the peaches to a large stone crock or wide-mouthed glass jar which has been scalded with boiling water. Add one cup of brandy and cover. Simmer remaining peach juice until it is reduced to half its original volume, then pour it into the crock. Cover tightly and store in a cool place for at least 3 days before serving. If stored for a longer time, add brandy as needed to keep the fruit covered with liquid. Apricots may be substituted for peaches.

12 large whole spiced
*   peaches, canned*
12 cloves
1 stick cinnamon
1 blade mace
1 cup brandy

Mincemeat Pie

Mix beef, suet, sugar, fruit, salt, spices, and cider in a large kettle. Cover and simmer, stirring frequently, for 2 hours. Add cider if needed. Stir in brandy to taste. Pack into sterilized 1-quart jars, seal securely, store in a cool place, and allow to mellow at least 1 month before using. Makes five jars.

To make the pie: Line a 9-inch pie pan with pastry. Spoon in enough mincemeat to fill the pan and cover with remaining pastry, rolled thin. Seal securely and slash top in several places so steam can escape. Bake in a preheated 450° oven for 30 minutes. Serve warm.

2 pounds lean beef, ground
1 pound suet, ground
2 pounds sugar
5 pounds tart apples
    (pared, cored, and
    chopped)
2 pounds muscat raisins
1 pound currants
1 pound sultana raisins
½ pound citron, chopped
½ pound orange peel,
    chopped
1 tablespoon salt
1 teaspoon cinnamon
1 teaspoon allspice
1 teaspoon mace
1 quart boiled cider (about)
brandy
pastry for a 2-crust pie

Apple Pie

Apple pie is what some things are as American as, and it has, in various forms, been eaten for breakfast, for an entree, and for dessert. Some of the first orchards in New England were planted by William Blaxton, a clergyman who owned, for a time, a farm on Beacon Hill. He moved to Rhode Island in 1635 and raised what is now called the Sweet Rhode Island greening—the first apple, as a distinct type, to be grown in the United States.

Prepare the pastry. Divide in half, line a 9-inch pie pan with one portion, and save the remainder for the top. Refrigerate both while you make the filling. Measure the sliced apples. You should have about 4 cups. Mix apple slices with sugar, salt, cinnamon (if you use it), lemon rind, and lemon juice. Arrange a row inside chilled pastry shell, about one-half inch from edge, and work toward center until shell is covered. Pile remaining slices on top. Dot with butter and cover with top crust, slashed in several places. Seal edges securely and crimp. Bake in a preheated 450° oven for 10 minutes. Reduce heat to 350° and bake 30 to 35 minutes. Five minutes before pie has finished baking, brush top with cream and sprinkle generously with sugar. Serve warm or at room temperature with Cheddar cheese or ice cream.

pastry for a 2-crust pie
4 large greenings (peeled,
    cored, and sliced very
    thin)
1 cup sugar
¼ teaspoon salt
½ teaspoon cinnamon
    (optional)
grated rind of ½ lemon
1 tablespoon lemon juice
butter
cream

Pastry for Pie Crust

Sift flour and salt together in a bowl. Cut in shortening with a pastry blender or two knives until mixture looks mealy. Sprinkle water over mixture (the less water you use, the better your pastry). Mix lightly with a fork, then work the pastry with your hands until it can be formed into a ball. Chill thoroughly. Divide in half and roll one portion at a time on a lightly floured board. Using light strokes, start in the center and roll toward the edge. When dough is about ⅛ inch thick, line a 9-inch pie pan, pressing pastry to bottom and sides. Refrigerate both parts while you prepare the filling.

To make pastry for a 1-crust pie: Follow directions given above, cutting the ingredients in half. To prepare a baked pastry shell, line a 9-inch pie pan with the pastry and bake in a preheated 450° oven for 12 to 15 minutes.

2 cups all-purpose flour
1 teaspoon salt
⅔ cup shortening
5 to 6 tablespoons ice water

Indian Pudding

Stir corn meal, a little at a time, into the hot milk and cook over low heat or in the top of a double boiler, stirring constantly, for 15 minutes, or until thick. Remove from heat. Mix together sugar, baking soda, salt, ginger, and cinnamon, then stir into the corn-meal mixture. Add molasses and cold milk, mixing thoroughly. Pour into a 1-quart casserole and bake in a preheated 275° oven for 2 hours. Serve warm with whipped cream and a light sprinkling of freshly grated nutmeg. Serves six to eight.

¼ cup corn meal
2 cups hot milk
¼ cup sugar
⅛ teaspoon baking soda
½ teaspoon salt
½ teaspoon ground ginger
½ teaspoon ground cinnamon
¼ cup molasses
1 cup cold milk
whipped cream
nutmeg

Martha Washington's Great Cake

"Take 40 eggs & divide the whites from the youlks," reads the original recipe, now in the archives at Mount Vernon, *"& beat them to a froth."* Beating the whites of forty eggs to a froth with a little bundle of twigs would give any modern cook pause. This adaptation calls only for the ingredients available to Mrs. Washington, including *"frensh"* brandy. The cake was served at Mount Vernon on Christmas, Twelfth Night, and other *"Great Days."*

Pick over raisins and currants and soak them in water overnight. Chop orange and lemon peel quite fine; do the same with the citron, angelica, and both kinds of cherries. Pour brandy over fruit, cover, and allow to stand overnight. The following day, sift together flour, mace, and nutmeg. Set aside. Work butter until creamy, then add *1 cup sugar*, a little at a time, beating until smooth. Beat egg yolks until thick and light, then beat in remaining cup of sugar, a little at a time, and the lemon juice. Combine with butter-sugar mixture. Add flour and sherry alternately. Stir in all the fruit and, last of all, fold in stiffly beaten egg whites. Pour the batter into a well-greased and floured 10-inch tube pan, a 10-inch Turk's-head mold, or 2 large loaf pans. Place pan of hot water in the bottom of a preheated 350° oven. Place cake pans in oven and bake 20 minutes. Reduce heat to 325° and continue baking 1 hour and 40 minutes for large cake; 40 minutes for loaf cakes. Cakes are done when a toothpick, inserted at the center, comes out dry. Turn out on rack to cool, then wrap in cheesecloth soaked in sherry (or brandy), and store in an airtight crock or tin for a month or more. If, during this mellowing period, the cheesecloth dries out, soak it again with the same spirits and rewrap the cake. Recipe makes about eleven pounds of Great Cake.

1 pound golden raisins
1 box (11 ounces) currants
*1 cup (8 ounces) candied
    orange peel*
*¾ cup (6 ounces) candied
    lemon peel*
1 cup (8 ounces) citron
*⅓ cup (3 ounces) candied
    angelica*
*⅓ cup (3 ounces) candied
    red cherries*
*⅓ cup (3 ounces) candied
    green cherries*
½ cup brandy
*4½ cups sifted all-purpose
    flour*
1 teaspoon mace
½ teaspoon nutmeg
*1 pound (4 sticks) softened
    butter*
2 cups sugar
10 eggs, separated
2 teaspoons lemon juice
⅓ cup sherry

EARLY AMERICAN AND VICTORIAN CHRISTMAS CAROLS

Peace on Earth

Dmitri Bortniansky (1752–1825) is the composer of the tune of the famous "Vesper Hymn," widely sung in the United States to the verses of Longfellow beginning "Now on land and sea descending." In 1869, W.J. Wetmore (dates unknown) supplied the tune with a Christmas text by Stephen Foster's friend George Cooper and published it as a song for home entertainment.

Hark! the Christ-mas bells are ring-ing, Ech-oed all __ the

earth __ a-round O, the glad-ness they are bring-ing, Love is in their mer __ ry sound.

2. Bells are sounding o'er the meadows,
Waking all to pure delight!
Fancy sees in deep'ning shadows,
Shepherds watching there by night!

3. Bells are sounding o'er the city,
Hark! their burden as we go:
"Give the poor their meed of pity!"
"Help them, 'mid the frost and snow!"

4. O, the time of sweet forgiving!
Glad be ev'ry heart today!
Lo! the Prince of Peace is living,
Smiling on our earthly way!

140

CHORUS

Lo! the — star in wond-'rous glo-ry, Beams in — yon-der sky a-gain;

Hark! the — ho-ly an-gels sto-ry, Peace on — earth, good will towards men,

Hark! the ho-ly an-gels sto-ry, Peace on earth,— good will towards men.

The Sleighing Glee

In the mid-nineteenth century, songs about sleighing, skating, and other winter sports were enormously popular, and dozens of pieces of sheet music appeared celebrating the excitement and conviviality of winter excursions. T.J. Cook (dates unknown) was one of many song writers who responded to the popular taste for musical sleigh rides. He published this glee, complete with jingling refrain, in 1859. It is equally suitable for solo voice and for a group of singers, large or small.

Swift-ly o'er the snow we go, Moon beams sparkle round;___ Hoofs keep time to mu=sic's chime,
Glide a- long with laugh and song, O'er the fleec-y snow;___ Swift - ly ride with friende be-side,

Mer -ri- ly on we bound. A - way! a- way! a- way we go, Mer-ri-ly o'er the
Cheer-i- ly on we go.

fleec- y snow, A - way! a- way! a- way we go, Mer-ri- ly on we bound.

The Mirth and Glee Carolers on Columbia's Main Street.
Photograph by Robert Westgate.

Courtesy Conner Prairie Pioneer Settlement

Merry Old Christmas

The secular joys of the season are celebrated in this unabashedly "popular song" of 1840 by the otherwise unknown Austin Phillips. It presents "Merry Old Christmas" as a Dickensian figure, associated with good food and drink, with kissing girls under the mistletoe, and with old-fashioned patriotic sentiment.

There is an old man whom we all of us know, With a mer-ry bald_ pate, and a beard white as snow, He

2. Our fore - fathers hailed him as we hail him now, With the ev - er green leaves round his ever glad_ brow, When

3. Good lack! what mad pranks the old jo-ker has seen, When the girls_ were entrapp'd neath the Missletoe_ green; But

knocks at the door, both of cot-tage and hall, And a right heart y welcome, re - ceives at them all, This

smok'd the oak ben - ches with good_ homely fare, Plum_ pudding, roast beef,_ stout "Oc-to-ber" so rare, He

why should we en - vy the .jol - ly years fled, We have eyes quite as bright_ and ripe lips quite as red. Our

Colonial Williamsburg Photograph

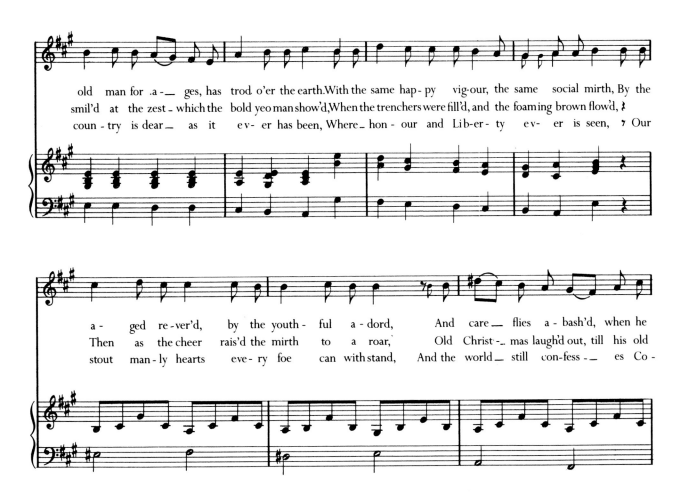

old man for .a -__ ges, has trod o'er the earth. With the same hap - py   vig-our, the same   social mirth, By the
smil'd   at the zest - which the bold yeo man show'd, When the trenchers were fill'd, and the foam ing brown flow'd,
coun - try is dear__ as it   ev- er has been, Where__ hon - our and Lib-er - ty   ev- er is seen, Our

a - ged re-ver'd,   by the youth- ful a-dord,   And   care__ flies a - bash'd, when he
Then   as the cheer   rais'd the mirth   to   a roar,   Old   Christ -__ mas laugh'd out, till his old
stout   man - ly hearts   eve- ry foe   can with stand,   And the world__ still con-fess -__ es Co -

sits at the board, Now who is this jol-ly old fel-low, I pray? who is_ this_ jol-ly old_
sides were_ sore, Who was the best friend of our fa-thers I pray? Who was_ the best friend of ·our
lum - bia the land. Then wel-come old Christmas to eve-ry heart dear, ⸵ Wel-come old Christmas to_

fel-low, I pray? Who but old Christ-mas, mer-ry old Christ-mas Dear to the heart as the
fa thers I pray? Who but old Christ-mas! Mer-ry old Christ-mas! Dear to the heart as the
eve-ry heart dear, Sing to old Christ-mas! Hap-py old Christmas! With hearts blithe and warm may he

sun to the day.
sun to the day.
long find us here.

Up on the Housetop

Benjamin R. Hanby (1833–1867) was called in his day the Stephen Foster of Ohio. His secular carol "Santa Claus," known today as "Up on the Housetop," was first published in the October 1866 issue of a children's periodical, Our Song Birds, *and over the years both tune and text have changed. This is the original version; it has not lost its vitality and exerts a quaint, often surprising, charm.*

Allegretto

1. Up - on the house, no de - lay no pause, Clat - ter the steeds of San - ta Claus;

Down thro' the chim - ney with loads of toys, Ho for the lit - tle ones, Christ - mas joys.

CHORUS

O! O! O! Who would -n't go, O! O! O! Who would -n't go,

Up - on the house top, click! click! click! Down thro the chim - ney with good St. Nick.

2. Look in the stockings of Little Will,
Ha! is it not a "glorious bill?
Hammer and gimlet and lots of tacks,
Whistle and whirligig, whip that cracks.

3. Snow-white stocking of little Nell,
Oh pretty Santa cram it well;
Leave her a dolly that laughs and cries,
One that can open and shut its eyes,

4. Pa, ma, and Uncle, and Grandma too,
All I declare have something new;
Even the baby enjoys his part,
Shaking a rattle, now bless his heart.

5. Rover come here, are you all alone,
Haven't they tossed you an extra bone?
Here's one to gladden your honest jaws
Now wag a "thank'ee" to Santa Claus.

CHRISTMAS CAROL

In 1850 Richard Stoors Willis (1819–1900) published his most famous tune in the New York Musical World. It was composed for the "Young Choristers of the Church of the Transfiguration" in New York, and Willis's choice of texts was the ever popular "While shepherds watched their flocks by night" of Nahum Tate. Here these words are replaced by the ones commonly used today; those who wish to sing the words that Willis chose can find them in Carr's "Hymn for Christmas" on page 00. (Nineteenth-century singers interchanged tunes and texts at will.) Slightly different from the one we know today, the tune is Willis's original, with his own ingenious and distinctive harmonization. The accompaniment is designed to provide four voice parts.

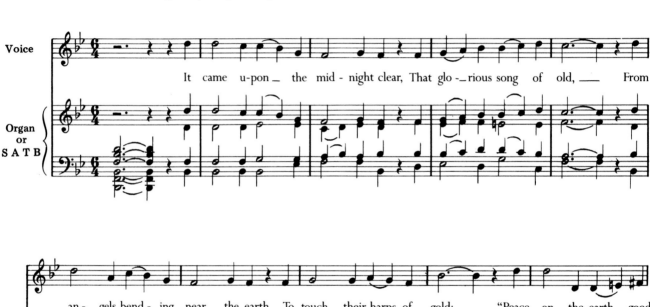

It came u-pon ___ the mid - night clear, That glo- ___ rious song of old, ___ From

an - gels bend - ing near the earth, To touch their harps ___ of gold: ___ "Peace on the earth, ___ good

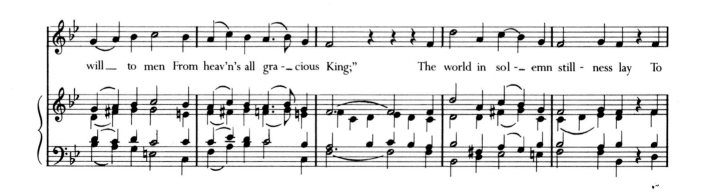

will ___ to men From heav'n's all gra- ___ cious King;" The world in sol- ___ emn still - ness lay To

hear the an - gels sing. —

Still thro' the clo - ven

skies they come, With peace- ful wings _ un- furled; _ And still their heav'n- ly mu - sic floats O'er

all the wea - ry world. _ A - bove its sad _ and low - ly plains They bend _ on hov -_ 'ring

wing, And ev - er o'er _ its Ba - bel sounds The bless - ed an _ gels sing. —

151

For

lo! the years are hast'- ning on, By proph - ets seen of old,____ When with the ev -_ er

circ - ling years Shall come the time_ fore - told,____ When the new heav'n_ and earth_ shall own The

Prince of Peace their King, And the whole world send back the song Which now the an -_ gels sing.__

FRANCE

Beginning in the 1820s, compilers and editors of hymnals included Christmas hymns and carols in increasing numbers as celebration of the holiday—frowned upon by the Puritan ancestors of Victorian Americans—burgeoned. Taken from The Dulcimer: or the New York Collection of Sacred Music *(Boston, 1850), this charming arrangement, from a French tune, by Isaac Woodbury (1819–1858) is typical of early American carols.*

Bright-est and best ___ of the sons ___ of the morn-ing,

Dawn ___ on our dark-ness, and lend ___ us thine aid; Star ___ of the

east, ___ the ho-ri-___zon a-dorn-ing, Guide ___ where the in-___ fant Re-

deem-___ er is laid, ___ Guide ___ where the in-___ fant Re-deem-er is laid.

2. Cold, on his cradle, the dewdrops are shining;
Low lies his bed with the beasts of the stall;
Angels adore him, in slumber reclining,
Maker and Monarch, and Savior of all,
Maker and Monarch, and Savior of all.

3. Say, shall we yield him, in costly devotion,
Odors of Eden and offerings divine?
Gems of the mountains, and pearls of the ocean,
Myrrh from the forest, and gold from the mine,
Myrrh from the forest, and gold from the mine.

4. Vainly we offer each ample oblation,
Vainly with gifts would his favor secure;
Richer by far is the heart's adoration,
Dearer to God are the prayers of the poor,
Dearer to God are the prayers of the poor.

A Hymn for Christmas

Benjamin Carr (1768–1831) was one of the first American composers to promote the performance of Christmas music in American churches. An important music publisher as well, he arranged the "Pastoral Symphony" from Handel's Messiah *as a Christmas carol in 1819.*

ti - dings of great joy I bring To ___ you ___ and all ___ man - kind. ___

CHORUS for Treble and Bass Voices

Al - _ le-lu - ia Al - _ le-lu - ia Al - _ le ___ lu _ ia

2. "To you, in David's town, this day
   Is born of David's line
   The Savior, who is Christ the Lord;
   And this shall be the sign:
   "The heavenly babe you there shall find
   To human view displayed,
   All meanly wrapped in swathing bands,
   And in a manger laid."

3. Thus spake the seraph; and forthwith
   Appeared a shining throng
   Of angels praising God, who thus
   Addressed their joyful song:
   "All glory be to God on high,
   And to the earth be peace;
   Good will henceforth from heaven to men
   Begin and never cease." A - men

SOURCE LIST

All the historic houses and villages featured in this book have their own gift shops, where reproductions of early Americana and Victorian Christmas items can be purchased.

Cooking for Christmas

The American Heritage Cookbook
American Heritage Publishing Co., Inc.
10 Rockefeller Plaza
New York, NY 10020

Connecticut à la Carte (Melinda M. Vance, ed.)
Connecticut à la Carte, Inc.
P.O. Box 17–158
West Hartford, CT 06117

Early American Holiday Recipes (free brochure)
Sleepy Hollow Restorations
150 White Plains Road
Tarrytown, NY 10591

The Williamsburg Cookbook: Traditional and Contemporary Recipes (compiled and adapted by Letha Booth et al.)
The Colonial Williamsburg Foundation
Williamsburg, VA 23187
Distributed by Holt, Rinehart and Winston, Inc.
521 Fifth Ave.
New York, NY 10175

Yuletide at Winterthur: Tastes and Visions of the Season
The Henry Francis du Pont Winterthur Museum
Winterthur, DE 19735

Decorating for Christmas

Colonial Williamsburg Decorates for Christmas: Step-by-Step Illustrated Instructions for Christmas Decorations (by L.H. Oliver et al.)
The Colonial Williamsburg Foundation
Williamsburg, VA 23187

The Decorated Tree: Recreating Traditional Christmas Ornaments (by C.E. Sterbenz, N. Johnson, G.A. Walther)
Harry N. Abrams, Inc.
100 Fifth Ave.
New York, NY 10011

The Gift of Christmas Past: A Return to Victorian Traditions (by Sunny O'Neil)
The American Association for State and Local History
708 Berry Road
Nashville, TN 37204

Christmas Food Items

Craft House
Box CH
Williamsburg, VA 23187
Source for Williamsburg Hams (by mail order).

Matthews 1812 House
Box 15
Whitcomb Hill Road
Cornwall Bridge, CT 06754–0015
Source for all-natural, home-baked gift cakes, including an heirloom-recipe fruit-and-nut cake.

Other Christmas Items

Bronson Imports
200 Fifth Ave.
New York, NY 10010
*Source for brass Christmas tree
ornaments, dolls with fine porcelain
heads.*

The Conemaker
1515 Jamestown Road
Williamsburg, VA 23185
*Source for wood cones with nails for
making fruit-pyramid table
centerpieces.*

Early American Life Magazine
P.O. Box 8200
Harrisburg, PA 17105
*Their annual publication
CHRISTMAS, as well as their
December issue, provide decorating
ideas, crafts (with step-by-step
instructions), and recipes for a
traditional holiday.*

Hartstone Inc.
P.O. Box 2626
Zanesville, OH 43701
*Source for stoneware cookie molds, with
recipes for gingerbread, anise
cookies, and cookie Christmas-tree
ornaments. Free brochure on
request.*

Museum of the City of New York
Fifth Avenue at 103 Street
New York, NY 10029
*Source for Victorian/Edwardian cards,
toys, ornaments, etc. EDWARDIAN
CHRISTMAS CATALOGUE, one
dollar for two years.*

Preservation Shops
1600 H Street NW
Washington, DC 20006
*Source for old-time reproduction
Christmas ornaments, toys.*

Shackman & CO./Merrimack
  Publishing Co.
85 Fifth Avenue
New York, NY 10003
*Source for Victorian toys, cards, seals,
gift wrappings, clip-on metal candle-
holders, etc., sold in shops
nationwide. Information available
from the New York office.*

The Smithsonian Institution
P.O. Box 2456
Washington, DC 20013
*Source for molded glass Christmas tree
ornaments, miniature American
flags (listed in Annual Fall
Catalogue).*

Williams-Sonoma
P.O. Box 7456
San Francisco, CA 94120–7456
*Source for English Christmas Crackers,
which snap when pulled by two
people, and a bay leaf Christmas
wreath (listed in their Christmas
Catalogue for Cooks)*

Keeping Christmas Greens

To make cut greens last throughout
the holidays out of water, harvest
your sprigs and cuttings the night
before you plan to decorate with
them. Crush the stem ends with a
hammer or make several long
vertical cuts. Place in a bucket of
cool water and leave overnight in a
cool basement or garage to absorb as
much water as possible. After
conditioning, dip holly stem ends in
candle wax to seal in the resin. Ivy
will last longer if you dip your entire
cutting (leaves and stems) in clear
liquid floor wax and spread on
newspapers to dry. With such
conditioning, boxwood and ivy
should last up to two weeks out of
water, holly, rosemary and bay to
ten days.
—*Early American Life*, December
1983, p. 41

RECIPE INDEX

ACKNOWLEDGMENTS

The Publishers wish to thank the following persons for their contributions to the book: recipe consultant, Michael Sonino; music engraver, Paul Sadowski of Music Publishing Services; donors to the cookbook *Connecticut à la Carte* whose recipes appear in Christmas Dinner with Mark Twain—Nancy Bailey, Diane Burgess, Alice F. Evans, Gloria Filhoff, Gloria J. Holtsinger, Bernice Kuzma, Eloise W. Martin, Gloria McDonagh, Kathleen J. Schwartz, Anne T. Shafer, Melinda M. Vance, and Joyce Anne Vitelli.

Appreciation should also be expressed for the invaluable assistance and encouragement of the staff personnel of the historic houses and villages featured in this book.

Karen Cure is a free-lance writer living in New York City. Her articles have appeared in many magazines, including *Harper's, Better Homes & Gardens,* and *Family Circle.* She has authored two travel books and has contributed to many others. She is a graduate of Brown University.

Neely Bruce is Associate Professor of Music and Director of Choral Activities at Wesleyan University. Composer, pianist, and conductor, he is internationally known as a scholar and performer of American music.